ies
introduces us to people in the Bible and shows how their lives have much to teach us today. All the authors in the series use their communication skills to lead us through the biblical record and apply its encouragements and challenges to our lives today. Every volume contains an *Index of Life Issues* to enhance its usefulness in reference and application.

By the same author:

What is Love?
Secret Warriors
To God be the Glory
Satanism and the Occult
Paganism and the Occult
Close Encounters with the New Age

CHARACTER AND CHARISMA SERIES

Joshua

Power to Win

Kevin Logan

KINGSWAY PUBLICATIONS
EASTBOURNE

First published in Great Britain 1998

ISBN 0 85476 744 4

Designed and produced by Bookprint Creative Services
P.O. Box 827, BN21 3YJ, England for
KINGSWAY PUBLICATIONS
Lottbridge Drove, Eastbourne, E Sussex BN23 6NT,
Printed in Great Britain.

Contents

To Linda –
my better half and research partner.
To Peter and Cathryn
and their future.

My Thanks

I went to pieces in my first three weeks at Oak Hill Theological College, London. I still shiver at the memory. In the years before as a journalist and sub-editor on an evening newspaper, I had dealt with page deadlines every forty-five minutes. Then, at college, I had twenty-one days to present my first essay – in New Testament studies. I didn't know what to do with so much time.

'We're expecting great things,' said one tutor. So, pride propelled me to read every library book on my subject. After twenty days, I had enough words for a dictionary. But there was no meaning. A thousand and one profound theological phrases floated in a fog.

It was five minutes to midnight on the day Christians should have been resting. The essay deadline was Monday breakfast. My mind was a dodgem track of religious ideas crashing senselessly into each other.

'I know,' a sudden brainwave hit me. 'I'll pray!'

Yes, I know some saints out there have this spiritual exercise well and truly wrapped up. And, yes, a theological student shouldn't need brainwaves to pray. But I still had 'L' plates on. (Psst! Still do!)

Anyway, within five minutes of sinking to my knees, I

had my subject mentally card-indexed and sub-edited into beautiful clarity. Before 2 am, I had it typed and stapled. On the front cover, I proudly printed my name.

'But what about the inspiration?' I thought. 'God's in every dot and comma.'

I therefore added '*+ the Lord*' after my name.

A few days passed before my essay plopped back into my college pigeonhole. Chris Byworth, only just beginning his sufferings as my New Testament tutor, was not at all impressed at having to mark a divinely inspired essay. In red ink, he wrote, 'Really! You're still only getting 56 per cent.'

Well, here I am, doing a repeat. It is an incredible honour to sit in front of a blank computer screen and say, 'Okay, Lord. Here we go again. Any good ideas?' And he always has. When I find myself stuck up a seemingly blind literary alley, I add, 'Why did you bring me here, Lord?' Always good to blame somebody other than yourself. Eventually, humility returns and I say, 'Lord, I'm lost. I hope you know the way out.' And he does.

The gracious Lord gets my first thanks. If you choose to give this effort only 56 per cent, well, I'm sure the Lord will cope. I'll sulk like mad, but I'll survive.

One hundred per cent support always comes from my much better half, Linda – that is, after I've followed her pencilled criticisms. She puts up with husbandless summers, except when I burrow out from the keyboard brandishing 'another chapter'!

I thank my lovely parish people at Christ Church, Accrington, for giving me an easy summer to write, and also those who stood in for me in various church ministries – Martin and Elaine Basden, John and Sheila Sanderson, Julie Jones and Paul Fountain. Great help also came from Betty Clegg, Marion Waite, Susan Hindle, Stephen Cox, David Graham, Geraint Williams, Vic Williams, Paul Waite, Marguerite Smith and Elaine Seymour. There are many other team players but I would need to publish half the church membership list to be fair. If this book sells a trillion, I'll remember you all in my will.

Sharon Lewis especially has my gratitude for her typing and extra research.

On the technical side, I have valued the excellent ministry of David Pawson (taped and live). I have long appreciated Alan Redpath and especially his book on Joshua, *Victorious Christian Living*. David Rhols' *A Test of Time* was a delightful help and John Drane is always excellent value, especially his *Introducing the Old Testament*. IVP's *The New Bible Dictionary* is the ever-present stand-by. There are also the writings of C.S. Lewis, Bishop J.C. Ryle, Francis Schaeffer and a hundred others right back to Enid Blyton! Do any of us, I wonder, ever write original stuff?

I have tried, wherever possible, to credit my sources of material. Sometimes, that is not possible. Ideas pop out – God-propelled, one prays. But I have to confess that original thought has never been my genius. I'm one of those who makes a brilliant discovery only to find somebody else invented it half a century ago. I'm for ever reinventing spiritual wheels, sometimes weeks after reading about them.

Finally, Linda and I have reached that very rewarding 'amnesic' stage of life. We forget we've seen good TV films and drama until sometimes the last few minutes of re-viewing them. It means we can enjoy them all over again. If I've done that with somebody's good theological ideas, my apologies. And my thanks to them.

Kevin Logan

Situations Vacant

Wanted: More Joshuas. No previous experience necessary. On-the-job-training provided. Candidates should be ready for life-changing adventure. They don't even have to be called Joshua. The original Joshua started out as Hoshea. Name changes can be arranged by divine appointment. Those interested in the power to win should read on.

A really useful reading tip . . .

Our Joshua saga races through at a popular pace. Story-loving brains might like to stick with the tale in normal print before delving into the special interest panels. But you're the boss . . .

I
Saviour?

Only Hoshea could detect the faint echo of terrified screams as they stood on the banks of the mighty River Jordan. The sounds came from yesterday. They came from the mouths of babes.

Only Hoshea's eighty-year-old senses were travelled enough to have heard first hand the death cries. The others with him – hundreds of thousands of men, women and children – could hear only the rushing voice of a river in flood at their feet.

Hoshea's inner eye must, once again, have replayed the tragic scenes of tiny naked forms sliding into the gaping fiery innards of a stone-hearted deity. Sometimes, the toddlers had been old enough to reach out and grasp the rough, sloping arms of a god called Molech on to which they had been ceremonially thrown; lambs who screamed and didn't want to be sacrificed.

In those instances, a minor priest would have to brave the heat himself. With a ritual stick, he would knock away stubborn, podgy little fingers, and give their owners a final push into the hungry inferno. This was no child abuse. This he did with the full blessing of all assembled worshippers, even the reluctant parents. Occasionally, a mother's throat would seize, her Middle Eastern wail stifled by the horror of finality. And it was at those times that Molech's fans might hear the last bleat of another sacrifice.

Child sacrifice

This was demanded by Molech, the god of the Ammonites, who were based east of Jordan. Other nature religions, like those in Canaan, borrowed the practice and the god, often for what they considered the best of motives, as we'll see in Chapter 3.

There are records of child sacrifice occurring in the area of Canaan, though at later periods. It was definitely practised in Jerusalem's southern valley of Hinnom (later used for burning rubbish and corpses; the Greek is *geena*, and in Latin, *Gehenna* – Jesus' synonym for hell).

Israel almost followed Molech during their wilderness wanderings but were warned against child sacrifice. Canaan had reached the depth of depravity when Joshua went spying, and so I have used the likely practice of child sacrifice to illustrate this.

The Source, James A. Michener's well-researched novel and sweeping chronology of Israel's history, is particularly helpful (Fawcett Crest, New York).

Hoshea peered across the river. He had been haunted by the corruption of the land beyond for longer than he could humanly bear. The screaming of little ones was just one focus of the evil. He now stood on the border of the hell where he had first heard them.

He had wanted to invade this land of Canaan ever since his spying days, half a lifetime ago. It was then that he and eleven other Israelite secret agents had been licensed by Moses to seek and find a strategy that would deliver God's Promised

Land into their possession. But what they had seen had so terrified ten of the spies that only Caleb and himself had urged Moses and his Israelites to invade (Num 13–14).

Giants abroad

We're not sure what sort of giants the ten spies saw and feared. There were certainly some large people in the lands of the Bible. King Og of Bashan's bed or sarcophagus was more than 13ft long and 6ft wide (Deut 3:11).

Goliath, around 9ft tall, was possibly one of the Anakim race of large people. They fled Hebron before the invading Israelites to settle in Philistine towns (1 Sam 17:4).

Those who now stood beside Hoshea on the banks of the swollen Jordan had heard only the legends. Most were less than forty years old and expert only in circling the desert. They had little experience by which to gauge these tales of foreign lands. True, there had been an occasional incidence of child sacrifice among their own tribes, but Moses and the sentence of death by stoning had put a halt to that (Lev 20:1–6).

The only cruelty their ears and eyes had had to endure was that normally inflicted by nature on any wilderness nomad. It was a hard existence, yet tempered always by willing, caring and giving human companionship. They were a people who had never holidayed abroad. Their education was simple, uncluttered by comparative religion. They had never felt the need for an equal opportunities policy nor political correctness. They didn't have to. They were one people offering opportunities to all, a single culture, a unified religion with theological correctness, Ten Commandments and one almighty God.

And quite a nice God, at that. A dedicated daily breadwinner who thought of everything. There was a delivery of heavenly manna food each morning, and even a double portion for the weekend. All could then have a relaxing day, himself included (Ex 16).

Manna from heaven

Sinai tree insects, such as cicadas, secrete honey-dew. This then dries to white flakes and falls from branches to the ground. Perhaps this was God's manna, according to one suggestion.

Another theory cites occasional falls of 'whitish, odourless, tasteless matter of a farinaceous kind which covered tents and vegetation each morning' (A. Rendle Short, *Modern Discovery of the Bible*, 1952).

There are other natural explanations but none really fit biblical descriptions (Ex 16; Num 11).

'The provision of manna remains ultimately in the realm of the miraculous,' writes Egyptian/Coptic expert K.A. Kitchen, 'especially in its continuity, quantity and six-day periodicity.'

To be sure, this God liked sacrifices, but only those which the people could well afford. And they never ever involved children's lives. Even the age-old circumcision rite of sacrificing a baby's foreskin had been quietly forgotten in the gynaecological wards of the wilderness (Josh 5:5).

Tales of baby sacrifice and the corruption of Canaan were hard to swallow for these wanderers of the wilderness, but they trusted their leader and their God. They had to.

Their parents had trusted only themselves. Their reward had been a death in a desert overflowing with misery and hopelessness (Josh 5:6). In fact, their parents had wanted to stone Hoshea and Caleb to death when, as spies, they had returned with their tall stories. As a consequence, their forefathers had forfeited a land overflowing with milk and honey. God had decided that only a new and a trusting generation would enter – they and the two spies, Hoshea and Caleb.

Stoning to death

Barbaric it may sound, but stoning was probably the most humane method of execution available to a Flint/Bronze Age people.

Normally, witnesses bringing the capital charges (at least two) had to cast the first stone. If done properly, this alone could bring unconsciousness, and even death.

Others in the community would join in the stoning to show that all had a responsibility for law and order. Joshua himself was to use it following a court hearing to execute Achan who placed the whole nation in jeopardy (see also Chapter 14).

Only Hoshea and Caleb were true to God. Only they had grasped that God prized obedience and trust above all else. Here was a God who would give his children anything he and they liked. All they had to do was accept him as the Boss.

Hoshea was to be trusted not only because he was God's man. He also had a track record second to none. He had been Moses' right-hand man for forty years and had helped him get the Ten Commandments on Mount Sinai (Ex 33:11). Before that, he had impressed even in the bondage of Egypt, becoming a tribal leader of Ephraim. It was this that had qualified him for the spying mission (Num 13:1–8). He had lived up to his family name, which meant 'saviour'. It was a popular Jewish first name for the sons of a people who yearned for such a being. True, Granddad Elishama was the big tribal chief (1 Chron 7:26–27), but among a people in desperate straits, leadership had to be based on skill and charisma rather than nepotism. Beyond the Exodus, Hoshea was the general who transformed a bunch of snivelling slaves into an army of extraordinary people. They sent the mighty Amalekites scuttling south for safety (Ex 17:8–16).

The people were certainly content with him as they faced an adventurous future. Only one person, in fact, had any doubts. Hoshea himself.

Two things stopped him turning tail and settling for anonymity in the wilderness. First, there were the memories which symbolised all that was rotten in the state of Canaan – the screams of the lambs. He desperately wanted those silenced. Second, the call of God which, at times, he also wished could be silenced.

Go and take the land!

Conquer the land, was the call. You shall be my servant, was the command. Easy in words. But in action, a mission humanly impossible. Ahead raged the Jordan in April flood, up to half a mile across in places. The hidden rip tides and whirlpools would decimate his three million followers. The land beyond was also overflowing with vicious regimes which butchered babies in their church services.

Counting by numbers

Our Old Testament numbers are lifted straight from today's Bibles. However, reliable biblical scholars advise caution.

We know that copying has caused some errors. For instance, 1 Chronicles 19:18 tells of 7,000 men dying while the same episode in 2 Samuel 10:18 records 700 deaths.

It's easy for us today to miss off a nought, but it was even easier for the scribes of old to miss a tiny line or speck in blurred ancient manuscripts. Some scholars are especially critical of the high Exodus numbers. The population of

Canaan was well below three million, according to reliable archaeological findings. Scripture, however, implies that the Israelites were 'the fewest of all peoples' (Deut 7:7), yet Numbers puts them around three million.

One possible solution may be in the translation of the Hebrew word for 'thousand'. It can also mean 'my tent group' or 'family'. This would considerably reduce the Israelites.

We should also realise that modern humanity is often left guessing at the Hebrew culture's handling of numbers. Many numbers are used symbolically. Six is the number of man. Seven stands for perfection and God. Forty is often used to denote a generation. The ancients would have been totally confused with the modern preoccupation with exact time (see also 'God's number' in Chapter 14).

God planned a beach mission of his own. He wanted to use this Mediterranean seaside strip as a universal stage for his divine drama. It was ideal for the task – a landbridge between the world's north and south civilisations. However, the production skills for such an epic would need to be of Oscar-winning proportions.

Forty years before, in the prime and full blush of youth, Hoshea had no such qualms. His fellow spies of that generation feared giants but he, along with Caleb, had assured Moses that God was big enough for the job. With divine help, they could do it.

Now Hoshea was not so sure. Then, there was Moses. Now there was just himself.

Moses might have been a wimp to start with. In more modern terms, he was more a dithering Frank Spencer in *Some Mothers Do 'Ave 'Em* than the heroic Charlton Heston. He suffered from Pharaoh-phobia. He stuttered and stammered. He was more at home with sheep than society. His

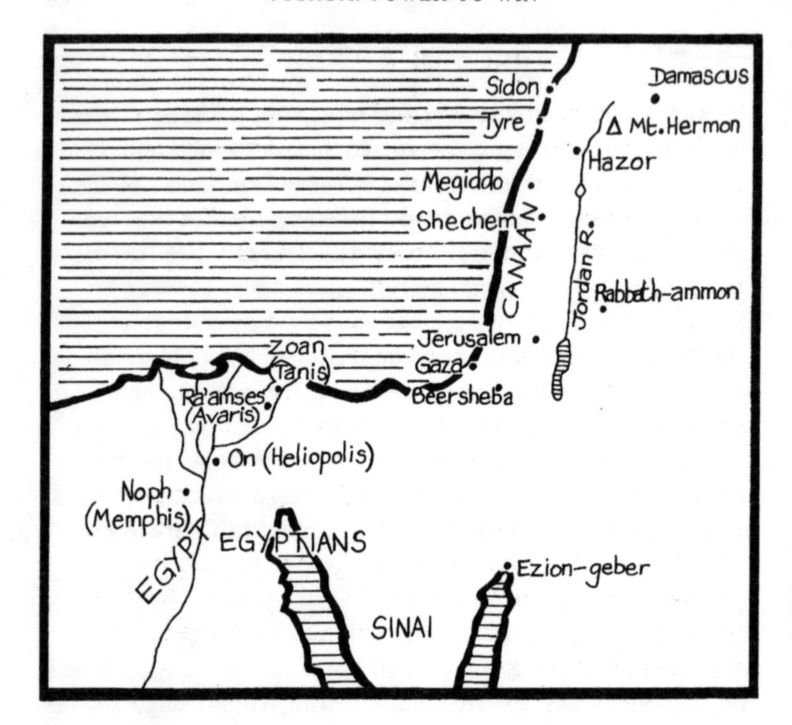

fears were the demons in his inner hell. But at least Moses had his burning bush. There was also the Great I AM God speaking out of it.

As if that wasn't enough, there was a miraculous package of divine tricks. This included a staff with a constant identity crisis. First it was a snake, trying to charm a Pharaoh into letting God's people go. Next it 'miracled' water into blood for one of Egypt's plagues. Then it became a divining rod, making water spring from solid rock in the desert. It was a baton held aloft to conduct military victories, and it could hold back the mighty waters of the Exodus sea (Ex 4:3; 7:17; 14:16; 17:5–7).

Hoshea thought that such a staff would be more than welcome here on the banks of a raging torrent. So would its Creator.

What's in a name?

Not much according to you and me today, except personal likes and dislikes. To the ancients, a name summed up the main role or character of a person.

Names used to be more than personal tags. Out of one of my windows I can look towards Oswaldtwistle. 'Twistle' used to be a stream, and this one marked the boundary of Oswald's northern kingdom. On the other side of the house is Ramsbottom. Now, don't get ahead of me. It was simply the valley floor where the rams grazed. It gives you the idea of how Israel used personal names.

God was very jealous of his name – Yahweh. It was not to be used in vain, according to the Commandments. It was not even to be used at all, according to the Israelites. The Great I AM was too holy. Gospel scribes had no problem writing the 'kingdom of God', except Matthew. He was writing for a mainly Jewish audience and called it the 'kingdom of heaven'.

Of course, there's a whole series of name changes in the Bible. Genesis' Abram meant 'exalted father'. Once God called him to sire his holy people he qualified as 'father of multitudes' – Abraham. Wife Sarai became Sarah 'mother of nations'. The barren couple chuckled over God's promise of a son with their old age pension. So he was called 'he laughed' – Isaac.

Hoshea was just a human saviour. Ya-hoshea was God's saviour. And that's how Jesus got his name. He was also Emmanuel, which means 'God with us'.

At one time, Moses had renamed his assistant Hoshea as Ya-hoshea – God's saviour (Num 13:16)! But surely a different name would not alter the dangerous game. There was still that river; still millions of bodies to transport across it. There were the same number of mouths to feed. Added to that were a million or so unknown, untried enemies beyond the river. All lived in fortified cities with hi-tech Bronze Age weapons of war and their chariots of iron. The wilderness Israelites were still in the Flint Age!

Strength and courage faltered. He was about to become either the biggest fool in Hebrew annals or one of their greatest heroes. Time and tide normally waited for no man, except perhaps a Moses.

But for a Hoshea . . . ?

Would the Great I AM God be with him as he was with Moses? A *no* would not only bring failure but add another haunting sound alongside the screams of children. . . . Waves of mocking laughter. A *yes* would mean, perhaps, the salvation of the world.

Would the waters really part for him as they had parted for Moses? Would mighty armies crumble before simple wandering nomads? How could they possibly penetrate centuries of fortifications?

Was he merely Hoshea, a human hope? Or was he, out of all people of all Old Testament ages, Ya-hoshea – God's saviour?

Joshua?

2
Saviour in the Making

A northern church had no reserves. Just mounting debts. Parishioners, on average, gave less than a packet of fags each week. Despite many appeals, hectic fund-raising, raffles and even a licensed lottery, it was losing £50 a week. Gaily coloured dry rot spores decorated a roof beam, and bankruptcy seemed the final destination. Some speculated that the newly appointed minister would be the last one. The vicar himself arrived at the same conclusion before long. He shared his doubts with God.

'Trust me!' the quietness of God seemed to reply. 'Stop the gambling. Shelve the money-raising efforts until the people stop robbing me [Mal 3:6–18]. Let them start to give me what is mine – a tenth of what I have enabled them to earn . . . .'

'But, Lord, this is the Church of England and the official line is only 5 per cent, and besides, these are Lancashire folk who – '

'. . . and what's more,' the quietness was louder, 'the church must immediately begin to give away a tenth of its own income to my work outside the parish.'

'But, Lord,' the stressed vicar stressed, not at all quietly, 'they'll think I'm crazy. They'll laugh in my face if I tell

them to stop raising money and give it away instead. They've stopped stoning vicars in these parts but who knows – '

'And who's to be in charge?' the quietness whispered. 'Your church or mine? My spiritual principles are not always the same as your business ones. Do it and just you see: I'll pour out so much blessing upon you that you will not have room for it all.'

* * *

Such is the Joshua dilemma in a modern setting and on a miniature scale. The circumstances are different. It's another age and another country, but sooner or later this challenge comes to each of God's people. Every one of us faces such decisions in our lives, and usually more than once. How we deal with these challenges often dictates at which level we live the spiritual life.

That northern church . . .?

The debt-ridden church broke even financially eighteen months after it started to give away part of its income and teach its members to tithe. The economic rot, and even the dry rot, was arrested.

Since then, the church has given thousands to missions and the Lord has made it his mission to bless it. It has thrived now for a decade.

'Test me in this,' says the Lord. He won't let us down.

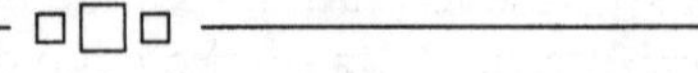

For Joshua, his D-day was fast approaching. It was time to start being God's saviour for the most crucial of Old Testament situations. The secret agents he had despatched behind enemy lines three days before had returned from

Jericho across the Jordan (Josh 2). Now, he must give his priests an order that appeared the height of human folly: 'Take up the ark of the covenant and pass on ahead of the people . . . when you reach the edge of Jordan's waters, go and stand in the river' (Josh 3:6, 8).

The ark of the covenant

The ark was the size of a packing trunk. It was made of acacia wood and coated inside with pure gold. The lid, a solid gold plate, boasted two cherubs with angelic wings spread for flight. They formed a visible throne for the invisible God.

Inside were the stone tablets etched with the Ten Commandments. There was also a pot of manna and that miraculous staff belonging to Moses and Aaron. Together, they reminded the people of just how well their God provides.

The ark was God's way of saying: 'I'm right here with you!'

What do you do when God makes his will crystal clear? The flesh-and-blood story of Joshua, like all of Scripture, is turned into black ink on white so that we might know the answer to these spiritual conundrums (2 Tim 3:16).

Come. Let us time-travel back into the years that led up to this Joshua dilemma. We might then know how to act in similar spiritual situations. Come to a land called Goshen, in the eastern Nile delta on the edge of the then mighty Egypt.

Joshua was the son of Nun, whose father was tribal chief. Nun and Mum, like most enslaved people, yearned for a saviour. Maybe it would be their son. What was needed was a rescuer from Egyptian overlords who often killed Hebrew boys at birth (Ex 1–2). Those who survived were forced to make bricks for the Pharaoh's great cities without having the right materials. Imagine having to make mud cubes without anything to bind the ingredients together (Ex 5:6ff). It was the final straw! A saviour had to be found.

Death by drowning

Hebrew baby boys were often about as valuable to the Egyptians as a bag of unwanted kittens. The Nile was the best place to toss them.

Not that it was a regular feature, for the Israelites were later to muster a fine fighting force in the wilderness. But it was the normal way of regulating an enslaved people.

It minimised rebellion, not to mention the food bill, especially among a people whose birds and bees thought they were rabbits.

Had Nun and Mum known it, their people's first saviour was already in the making. It was about the same time that they named their child 'saviour'. A prince called Moses had slain an Egyptian for abusing a Hebrew slave. It was his own hot-headed human attempt at being a saviour. There were witnesses, so he fled into the wilderness in fear of his life. God had to take this royal somebody and turn him into a wilderness nobody before he could retrain him.

And alongside this, the fashioning of the one who was to become Moses' young assistant-cum-successor had also begun.

His education

Like any good Jewish boy, Joshua was brought up on the three 'A's – Adam, Abraham and that Amazing multi-coloured dreamcoat of Joseph's. God's creation was perfect in Adam and Eve. Then the new humans changed God's fixed menu for life into à la carte. They grew tired of being told what they could and couldn't eat. Eve, with a nudge from the serpent, tasted the forbidden fruit, followed rapidly by hubby. In that spiritually fatal moment, they became their own gods. Their actions indicated precisely where the Almighty should go – out of their lives.

And that was the original sin.

Other not-so-original sins flooded in and so did God's anger. As we know, only Noah and his family survived. Within years of their ark settling on dry ground, humanity was as bad as ever. A man from Ur (in present-day Iraq) called Abram – a friend of God's – became humanity's hope.

'Leave your country . . .' commanded the Lord, 'and go to a land I will show you. I will make you into a great nation and I will bless you' (Gen 12:1–2).

A 2,000-mile emigration trail began just after 2000 BC. It brought him and his family to the great trees at Shechem and Hebron (the geographical York and London of what was to be the Promised Land). In the north, Abraham learned that the land would be his after the then occupants' sin had 'reached its full measure' (more of this in Chapter 3).

In the south, his elderly wife, Sarah, had a good chuckle on overhearing that her octogenarian husband was about to give her a son (Gen 18:1–15). God, however, had the last laugh and began the biblical 'begatting'. Out popped Isaac first, and he bred the Hebrews. That started with the terrible twins, Jacob and Esau. Jacob did a whole lot of 'begatting', and one of his dozen sons was his favourite, Joseph.

Jacob was so fond of his eleventh son – his first by his first love Rachel – that he spoiled the lad, much to the disgust of the others. The gift of a multi-coloured coat made the jealous brothers see red and they sold poor Joseph into

Egyptian slavery. Despite this distinct disadvantage, he rose – miraculously, it has to be said – to high office. A touch of divine intervention and a bit of good forward planning enabled him to save the nation from a seven-year famine. When his old family came scrounging for food he eventually found it in his heart to forgive them. The Hebrews subsequently moved into Goshen but became so numerous that racial fears caused Egyptian leaders to rise up against them. Slavery became Egypt's answer to its immigration problem (Ex 1–2).

Old Testament holocaust

The happy ending of Joseph and His Amazing Technicolor Dreamcoat lasted only for a generation.

Enter Adolf Hitler Mark I, complete with mini holocaust. He and succeeding Pharaohs saw the Jews as a threat to their master Egyptian race, ruthlessly subjugating them by slavery and controlling them with male infanticide (Ex 1).

Adult male slaves couldn't very well be drowned in the Nile like children, so Pharaoh Adolf and his ilk burned, whipped and worked many to death under the blazing Egyptian sun. When upstart Moses had the audacity to demand freedom, they really did become a stench that had to be eradicated at all costs (Ex 5).

Had God not intervened with his ten plagues, the Jewish story would never have become the world best-seller it is today. The Jews wouldn't even have rated an historical footnote.

Incidentally, slavery was not always bad news. It was often a life-saver. Prisoners of war, for example, could opt for service or summary execution. Those who fell behind on the HP payments could become unpaid domestics rather than chance the debtors' dungeons that only gave up their dead.

There was even DIY slavery. Those who couldn't cope with the cost of living could volunteer for slavery. Better to serve than starve. The Israelites occasionally thought this during the early wilderness trials. But not for long.

The foundation of our Joshua character was in these Eden to Egypt stories. As he stood on the banks of the swollen Jordan he knew certain truths. They were chosen men and women. They belonged to a chosen race. They had a divine future, and it looked increasingly certain that he did too. The God who did the choosing was in charge of world-shaking events such as the creation and the Flood. He was a King who took risks by giving his subjects free will. Yet, he still went on loving them when they deposed him.

An almighty, never-say-die kind of loving kept nudging, calling, cajoling, and courting his loved ones. The One who had the power over nations and even Pharaohs cared for small clans and tribes. The One who determined who would rise and fall, possessed a patience that was eternally elastic. This was a God who had power over the shrivelled-up womb of a sceptic called Sarah. He could even give an old age pensioner a bouncing baby boy.

Surely, Joshua reasoned, such a God could handle a mere raging river!

Couldn't he?

The Exodus

Joshua's secondary education began the day Moses arrived back in town. Moses came riding in with Aaron and his miraculous staff. Joshua, approaching forty but still a youth according to the Old Testament, became the great man's number one assistant (Num 11:28).

Young or old

The Bible knows nothing about the middle-aged. You are either young or old.

Youth is Old Testament shorthand for people who still have their own teeth and hair colour (for example, Proverbs 20:29).

Incidentally, a touch of grey by no means implied that you were past it. Quite the opposite. Toothless greys were the wise ones (quite right, too!).

Imagine the learning insights of such a position:

- Involved first hand in Egyptian court affairs as Moses pleads for God's people to be released;
- Observing the hardening of a Pharaoh's heart despite Moses and his marvellous and miraculous staff;
- Witnessing the Nile turn to blood, a farce of frogs, a dust-storm of gnats, fly-filled houses, BSE in the beef, a skinful of boils, battering by football-size hailstones, farms stripped by locusts and a darkness that the Egyptians could almost feel;
- Seeing an angry God make Egypt cry as his angel of death claimed their first-born;
- The relief of God's wrath passing over the Hebrew homes, protected by daubs of blood from sacrificial lambs (Ex 7–12);
- Finally, seeing the waters of the Exodus sea, east of Goshen, suddenly part and wall up on either side of the migrating people (Ex 13:7–22).

The Exodus sea

Which sea was it?

The modern Red Sea becomes the Gulf of Suez and stops at Suez, dozens of miles below where the Exodus crossing was supposed to have taken place. North of Suez and about thirty miles below Port Said on the Mediterranean there are the Bitter Lakes, on the present route of the Suez Canal.

The Red Sea (*yam sûp̄* in Hebrew) of Scripture is these lakes (*yam sûp̄* translates to 'sea of reeds/weeds'). It is possible that the Bitter Lakes were thought of as remote extensions of the Red Sea in ancient times, though there is no evidence for this.

The Bitter Lakes are affected by the 'strong east winds' mentioned in Exodus; they also border on Shur, the area Israel entered after crossing the *yam suph* (K.A. Kitchen, *The New Bible Dictionary*).

To save confusion, I refer to the sea as the Exodus sea.

As Joshua thought back on all these things, the flooding River Jordan again seemed to shrink a little. It was comforting to remember what God had done. If only the Lord would be with him as he was with his old boss.

The exploring

We now move on to Joshua's Sandhurst or Westpoint: his military education. The Amalekites were perhaps the first sign to Joshua that God was personally with him.

'Choose some of our men,' Moses commanded him, 'and go out to fight the Amalekites' (Ex 17:9).

The Amalekites

They were descended from Esau, the twin who sold his inheritance and divine blessing to brother Jacob for a bowl of food. Amalek was Esau's grandson.

Because of the Amalekites' attack on Israel, they came

under divine censure and were to be destroyed (Deut 25:19). The memory of them would be blotted out from under heaven.

It was an incredible day. First they were winning, then the battle flowed against them. Regrouping, they flung themselves forward once more and managed to hold out until sunset when they 'overcame the Amalekite army with the sword'. It was a glorious day. It was the Lord's day. Surely, it was Joshua's day, too.

But then came the battle despatches, and they painted a different picture.

'Write this on a scroll,' said the Lord, 'as something to be remembered, and make sure that Joshua hears about it.'

And what was written down made it a day belonging more to Moses and the Lord rather than Joshua. It turned out that Moses was up a nearby mountain, once again with that miraculous staff of his, holding it aloft for victory. The times Joshua felt the battle slipping were the times Moses' arms got tired and his staff lowered. And then it turned out that the only reason Joshua had scored his victory was because Aaron and Hur sat Moses on a stone stool and held up his arms until sunset.

And here Joshua was now at the Jordan. No Moses. That staff locked away in the ark of the covenant. And the river still raged and gurgled laughingly at him.

And maybe so, too, would the people tomorrow.

One thing that carried Joshua forward was the belief that the sin and abominations and corruption of the Canaanites and Amorites had surely reached their full measure (Gen 15:16; Amorite is often used to mean those in Canaan).

He had seen enough to convince him that the occupants should be wiped off the face of the earth. Either that, or they would corrupt his people.

If that happened, then the drama that God intended to be played out on his world stage would be just another X-rated show. This was to be a clean sweep. A fresh start. God might once have painted his rainbow promise in the sky. Certainly, he wouldn't flood the world again. But that didn't mean he couldn't make an example of one small strip of land.

Hard though it was, every last man, woman and even child would have to be totally eliminated. Joshua had few qualms about doing that after what he had seen.

3
Parable from Hell

A picture is worth a thousand words. Painting a picture in people's minds with a parable cannot be far behind. Jesus used them to create vivid images for his followers.

Here then, in parable form, is a society whose sin has 'reached its full measure'. We briefly take leave of Joshua and his people and travel ahead of them over the Jordan. We taste the hell of Canaan, a corrupt state in moral decline for centuries.

Actually, we might not be too surprised with what we find. The Canaanites were not demons. They weren't even monsters of evil. They were human beings. Not too remote from us. Alarmingly, their actions and motives were not much different from ours today . . . .

The time and setting of our parable? Let's just say it was some time before Joshua arrived at the Jordan.

* * *

Hiel's land had once overflowed with milk and honey, but not any longer. And all for the want of a few raindrops. About the only thing that did drip – and it did so incessantly – was his wife's acid tongue.

'The kids need new sandals,' Ashtor's nagging always began thus, ' . . . and how much longer have I got to wear this rag you call a dress, and these jars – just how am I expected to draw from the well with cracked pots . . . ?'

This was usually the cue for the leather-skinned farmer to mumble his excuses and leave.

'That's right, skulk off to your temple prostitutes,' Ashtor shrilled in his wake, 'and a fat lot of good they'll be. If you ask me, their goddess is as thick as two short planks and about as fertile as a frigid catfish.'

'Blasphemy!' Hiel turned on her, but only half-heartedly. Privately, he had entertained similar thoughts himself in recent months. He and his fellow Canaanites had this theory that a divine prostitute a day would keep the drought at bay. A touch of sympathetic magic, you might say. Another culture might curse their enemies by sticking pins into doll-like effigies. Not the Canaanites. For a start, they were after blessings. And rather than stick pins into prostitutes, they preferred more enjoyable methods. To us, it might sound like a great excuse for sex on demand, and for many a nominal Canaanite that's just exactly what it was. But not for farmer Hiel. The temple prostitute was as essential to his farming methods as his plough. With the metal tool he roused the earth. With the physical one he tried, with the assistance of the temple ladies, to inspire the god and goddess of fertility to reproduce life in the earth. This year, nothing had worked. All Hiel got was the magic of sex. For a farmer, it wasn't enough.

The various festival orgies hadn't helped either. Even Ashtor herself had tried a male prostitute or two. She'd prayed. She'd pleaded with this Baal. She'd prostituted herself. She'd had enough. Now, as far as she was concerned, there really was only one thing left for her people to do.

Get a new god!

They needed one with more power; more control over the

wind and the rain. True, appalling sacrifices were demanded by other gods, but times were getting desperate. New life in the earth was vital. The family had to survive, even if it meant sacrificing one of their number. Even the death of their youngest – the baby.

Life in the earth was scarce. If new life could be bought from cruel gods, then the necessary currency had to be found.

'And anyway,' Ashtor had begun to reason, 'children are easier to replace than the harvest.' The sacrifice of a child would be hard, but at least the rest of the children would thrive as a result.

Five years now, the drought had lasted. The ensuing famine and poverty brought weakness, and that invited invasion in a land that knew almost as many suitors as a temple prostitute. There were, for instance, the Egyptians from the south. The Hittites and then the Assyrians from the north. In between, the Phoenicians by the sea invaded inland. Empires swapped this postage-stamp size nation like schoolboy traders in the playground. And when the big 'mights' of empires rested, then the little 'ites' squabbled over it – Amorites, Perizzites, Hivites, Jebusites and the Girgashites.

From a geographical, agricultural and trading viewpoint, Canaan had the best site in the world. It consequently had the worst sights – war, treachery, murder and mayhem. In the lulls between, religion reigned, but it was still far from peaceful. 'Sunday' morning services included weird occultic nature worship, sex orgies and child sacrifice.

The day Hiel and Ashtor got married life looked like it might take a turn for the better. Their match was a good omen, and villagers for miles around came to celebrate. Hiel meant 'El lives', El being the chief Canaanite god. Ashtor's name sprang from the same source from which came Canaan's mother goddesses – Ashtoreth or Astarte. Yet another was Asherah, and she was actually the consort of El. Surely, such a marriage must be made in heaven.

On many subsequent high festivals and celebrations, the couple were the honoured guests, even though El and Asherah were not directly worshipped. They were, after all, the unapproachable high and mighty deities who subcontracted the human race to lesser beings – like Baal and his lover, Anat.

Baal, on the other hand, was much more immediate. He was the nature god of the weather, the one who quelled frightening storms and supplied life-giving rain. Why bother with a remote and transcendent deity when you could have intercourse with the god who really counted?

Annual resurrection

There was only one problem. Baal died every year. He had to. That was the only possible explanation for why the rains dried up from May to September, and why the sun baked the farm into a desert. Surely, if the Lord Baal had remained alive, he would have provided for his subjects all year round. The one who killed him was obviously opposed to life and all that Baal represented. He was Mut, the god of barrenness and sterility.

After harvest each May, the worshippers were left with no alternative but to join El and Asherah for their annual summer wake following Baal's death. At the same time, they pleaded with Baal's lover, the goddess of fertility, to seek her revenge. Once roused, the wrath of Anat knew no bounds. Annually, at the end of August, she captured Mut and made mincemeat out of him with a knife and shovel. She burned him. She ground him with millstones and fed his remains to the birds. Anat then brought Baal back to life through the power of their sexual relationship in time to provide the September rains. Mut was left to lick his wounds, and spent the whole winter pulling himself together in readiness for the cycle beginning again.

As each growing season approached, farmers like Hiel

would plough their land and plant their seeds. They would then visit the temple prostitutes to remind Anat and Baal to fertilise nature once again.

For the fifth year in succession, Anat and Baal were being distinctly coy. Or thick. Ashtor was now saying this publicly, severely criticising the gods for their poor productivity. Hiel was privately thinking of sacking them. But who would then fill the vacancy? Ashtor had already made up her mind.

'The new god has to be Molech!' Her face was set as granite.

Hiel was horrified. Sex orgies were not for Molech. His appetite demanded babies, toddlers, children. Usually the first-born who needed to be in perfect condition and often from the best families.

The ones who originally discovered Molech, the Ammonites (in present-day Jordan), had learned to their cost that this terrible god did not appreciate society's cast-offs. He demanded far more than the family runts; more perfection than the disabled. Not even the sons of poor families were good enough for him. The Ammonites had first offered their dross but the rains still did not fall. Obviously only the best would be acceptable.

The Ammonites

Ammon's grandfather was Lot, the nephew of Abraham. The Ammonites lived on the east bank of the Jordan, near where the Israelites crossed into the Promised Land.

Because they both had Abraham as their forefather, both the Ammonites and the Israelites considered themselves related and were on friendly terms. Indeed, Israel was commanded not to harass or provoke them to war because of God's blessing on the descendants of Lot (Deut 2:19).

There was trouble later when the Ammonites helped

those who were not on Israel's party list – the Moabites (Judg 3:13). During Israel's wanderings, the Ammonites must have encouraged some tribes to follow Molech.

Moses had to command Israel not to sacrifice their children (Lev 18:21).

For Hiel and Ashtor, and the whole community, conversion to this demanding god was not easy. In fact, the Ammonites had Molech to themselves for most of history, and it was only in times of great drought or when the priesthood was particularly sadistic that others in the Middle East entertained child sacrifice.

Before parents aborted their children in Molech's incinerators, there were certain conditions that had to be fulfilled. It had to be agreed that tribal or family health was at risk, mainly through the effects of drought. It had to be agreed that the sacrifice of a baby would be beneficial to them.

Modern sacrifice

In the year of writing, the number of babies aborted in the UK alone rose by 8.3 per cent to 177,225.[1] The total number of babies legally aborted since 1967 is 4.8 million.

It is increasingly acknowledged that the vast majority of the 470 babies aborted each day are sacrificed for convenience. The prime motive appears to be similar to Molech's day – to improve the quality of life for the mother and/or the remainder of the family.

In Canaan, babies were sacrificed during rituals lasting several days. In the UK, you can now do it in your lunch break.

The total number of babies sacrificed by the cultures condemned by God probably did not add up to the number we abort in a single year.

□□□

Poverty or a poor lifestyle could also be taken into consideration. Officially, you couldn't sacrifice babies on demand. That was illegal. However, more priests than not liked a quiet life, and would bow before a few well-timed tears. In some large families, sacrifice was more than welcome. It meant the loss of an extra mouth, especially a noisy one.

Five years without water. What would Hiel do?

To be sure, there were other beliefs and other alternatives. Hiel's namesake god, El, was after all supposed to be the boss. Somebody must be in charge somewhere. It was rather obvious to anybody with eyes that somebody must have caused the world, designed it, and then provided human intelligence. It wasn't intelligent to think that human intelligence came from non-intelligence. Who placed the lights in the sky? Who kept them there and moved them accordingly to what appeared to be set laws (Rom 1:18–32)?

Was it the one who created the world and then flooded it? Everybody knew that story, no matter from which country or culture they came. Traders told their version en route to the spice markets of Syria and the north. Travellers had different tales with different actors but it all boiled down to one El – an El who was almighty. One who was in charge.

El-Shaddai, some called him.

In the hope of peace and perhaps an end to the nagging, Hiel pushed away all these heady '-ologies'. He was a down-to-earth man, into agriculture, not theology. He eventually gave in to Ashtor. They settled on sacrificing their two youngest. Other families also made contributions, as they called them.

Hiel even managed a smile as he watched the first of his screaming children slide down the sloping arms of an impotent stone god called Molech. He stifled a scream as the last whimper of his last-born died in the flames within the god's clay stomach.

Molech, after all, expected a cheerful giver.

God the Revealer

Our own senses give more than a strong hint that something is out there. This 'something' gave the game away when visible beings and things like us and the universe were caused to appear.

There are said to be three possible causes for our existence. A Creator, chance, or that the universe, in one form or another, has always existed. For many, it demands too much blind, unsupported faith to believe that the beauty and complexity of life is a mere accident. The idea about matter/universe always existing is unprovable, unknowable and hard to credit. Many still want to ask, 'But what was or is the cause?'

Millions choose to say that there is a cause who is also a designer. He is also a giver of intelligence. And this makes the something into a Somebody.[2]

This is the Bible's stance. The act of creation tells us so much about the Creator. He is immensely large, powerful, eternal (because he has to have created time as well as space). He is also totally different from us. He is a Creator and we are creatures.

Apostle Paul puts it well in Romans 1:18 onwards. The invisible God's presence is shown by the glory that is visible. This is how even the Canaanites ended up with El. El was simply the word used to describe this Big Somebody.

So then, this God has revealed himself through the natural world.

Now, if we humans are left to ourselves at this point, we begin to make up the character of this Large Somebody from our fears, hopes and appetites.

Our fears make gods who must be bought with sacrifices, such as Baal, Molech and most pagan deities. Human hopes produce the secular religions like atheism, humanism and Marxism. We are our own gods and we can cope on our own, thank you very much.

Our appetites drive us to one of two extremes. If we feel guilty about them, we join the sects and cults to cleanse our souls lest the wrath of God gets us. Those who feel good about their appetites will be tempted to design a god who also likes them. That god can be anything from a New Age goddess to a lovey-dovey, anything-goes Jesus Christ.

This God business gets so messy because we are faulty creatures (sinners, for short) while God is perfect, totally different from us in that key respect.

Therefore we need more revelation. Without it we're in a mess.

God realised that, so he made his Word become flesh in his Son. And more. He inspired over forty writers in three continents and languages, over a period of 1,500 years, to set down his Word in words.

Just a thought: imagine a god who simply created us and the world and then came to a full stop. He neither sent us instructions in flesh and blood, nor in ink.

What Father would send his children into this crazy, dangerous world without full instructions and guidance? It would be a lousy parent who did that to his children.

It would be the very devil himself.

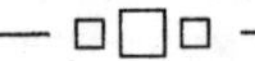

Notes

[1] Office of National Statistics, 1977.

[2] Professor Keith Ward's *God, Chance and Necessity* (Oneworld) is excellent.

4
God's No Devil

'Now then, you and all these people, get ready to cross the Jordan River into the land I am about to give to them – to the Israelites. I will give you every place where you set your foot, as I promised Moses. Your territory will extend from the desert to Lebanon, and from the great river, the Euphrates – all the Hittite country – to the Great Sea on the west. No-one will be able to stand up against you all the days of your life' (Josh 1:2–5).

* * *

Joshua has his holy orders: 'Go to war!'

'To where?' Mr Modern Man gasps incredulously.

'To war!' echoes the Old Testament.

'So primitive!' the sophisticated mouth tuts. 'How utterly barbaric! Senseless!'

Perhaps before accompanying Joshua on his warpath, a God test may help us.

His God and the air-conditioned deity designed for our third millennium appear to be somewhat at odds with each other. War!? Such an uncouth and violent order would never sully the lips of the modern happy-pappy sky-squatter.

The Promised Land according to the scriptural promise (Josh 1:2–5), *realised fully under King David*

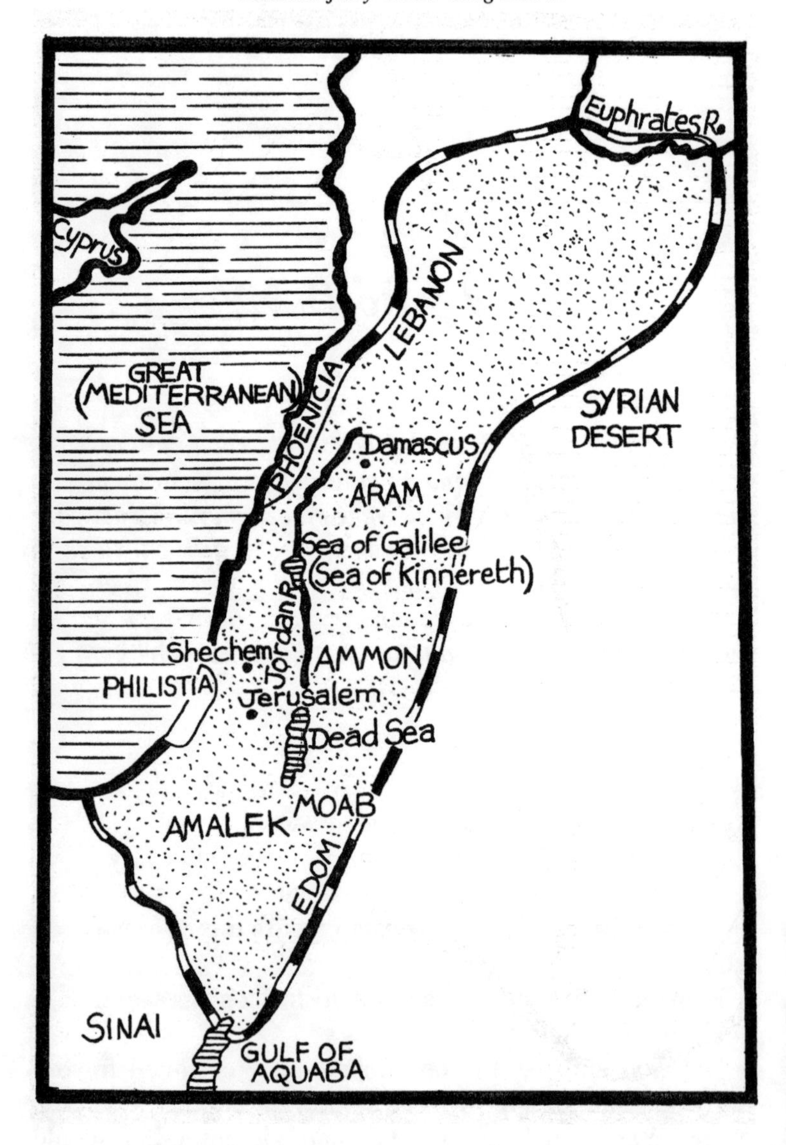

Canaan, the Promised Land which Joshua was about to enter

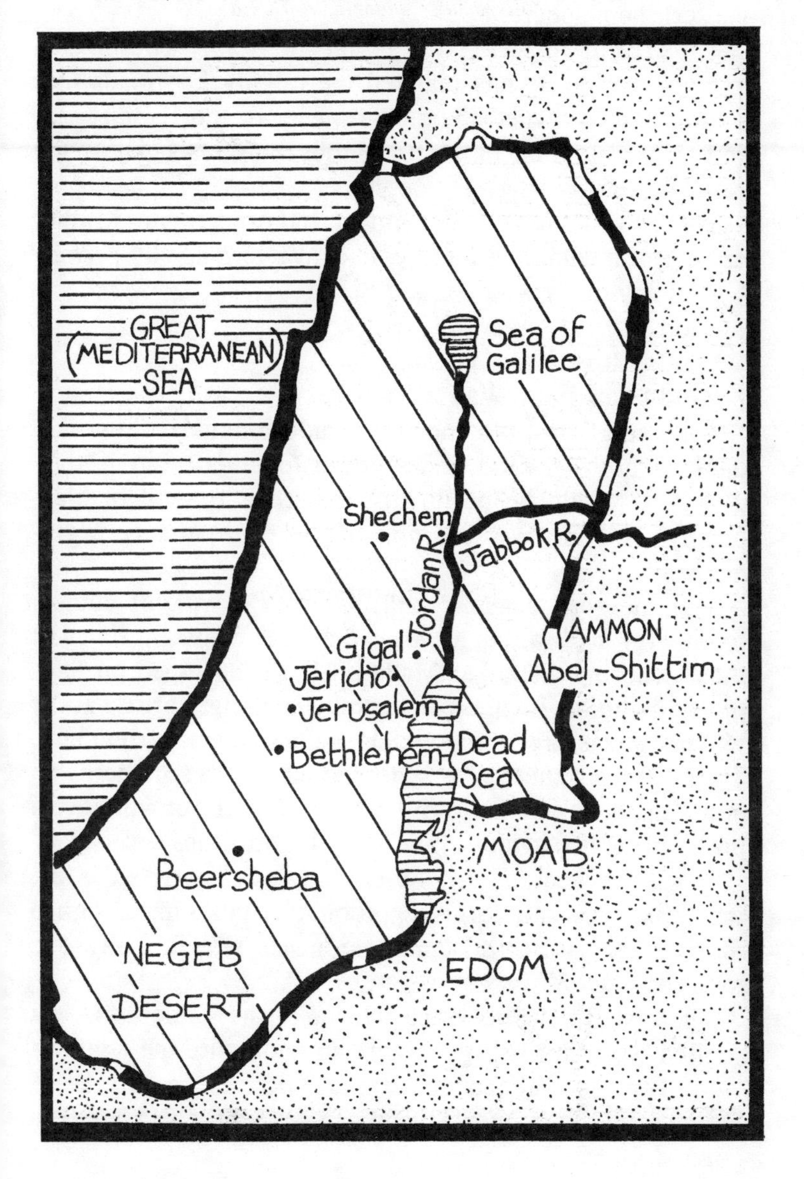

Heaven forbid! And, if not heaven, then certainly earth's western hemisphere.

The size of Joshua's God is uncomfortably awesome in today's world. He has plagued the mighty Egyptians into submission, drowned their charioteers in the Exodus sea, and then waged an ugly and bloody holy war against the Amalekites.

The god of the age of comfort and computers is rather more sentimental and cuddly, and, Western apathy permitting, many of us would chant:

'God is good / War is bad.'

'God is love / War is hate.'

'God gives life / War takes it.'

Such equations, our modern minds conclude, show that there is no way God and war go together. And if they did, both would be politically incorrect. A modern blasphemy! Not the Western god of the ever-patient, forgiving smile.

The 'no-god' brigade – the atheists – will, of course, foam over such a dangerous fantastical deity. So too will those whose gods have 'Made on Earth' stamped on their plastic bottoms. Even some churchgoers might bristle at the violent adventure upon which we are about to embark. Those, for instance, who last encountered the divine as an emasculated, meek-and-mild Sunday school wet will have a problem or two with Joshua's God. Ditto those who worship a white-bearded, eyes-a-twinkling deity. He's the one who, like any old forgiving fool, can be conned with a phoney tear and a sad complexion. He wouldn't say boo to a goose let alone go to war.

There will also be those who take the Bible as God's written word but still genuinely struggle with the wrath of God. They feel alienated from an Old Testament God of holiness and judgement, failing to see where the love has gone.

Finally, there are those who live at the level of constant

sainthood. The halo around their lives keeps at bay that nasty doubting world. They always let God be precisely as he appears to be in his Book. They ignore any hint of inconsistency. They continually accept his image and change their own to match his. They let God be God. Their reward is to escape to the next chapter.

As for the rest, we have to come to terms with a blood-curdling list of battle orders:

- Death sentence for deserters and rebels (Josh 1:18);
- Dispossession for those in the land (Josh 3:10);
- Fatal curses for any who rebuild Jericho city that is about to be demolished (Josh 6:26);
- Death by stoning for the greedy (Josh 7);
- Slaughter of 12,000 men and women (Josh 8:25);
- Public hanging for five kings (Josh 10:16–26);
- A 'shoot to kill' policy, destroying all who breathe (Josh 11:11);
- Annihilation for thirty-one kings and their realms (Josh 12:8–24).

I used the Book of Joshua as bedtime reading for my two primary-aged children many years ago. I wanted them to meet a God who loved them, and the whole world so much that he sent his Old Testament children on a salvation mission.

Here was a land already soaked in the blood of sacrificed children. It was the world's Red Light district in which everybody used God's beautiful gift of sex to couple themselves with made-to-measure gods, designed to meet their own selfish appetites or fears. There was incessant tribal warfare in which only the fittest survived, and Canaan's serial killing-fields were forerunners of our Bosnias and Rwandas today.

God and sex

'Go forth and multiply,' God ordered. But how did he dream up such a delightful multiplication method?

Consider his thinking. The brain he had figured out. The heart ticked well in his heavenly laboratory. Kidneys, livers, and so on, were perfected, and the eye fine-tuned. But how to duplicate it all? And repeatedly? Creator he was, but he was also Sustainer and Father. He was going to have his hands full.

Now, he could have been a kill-joy and installed a baby button behind Eve's left ear, labelled 'Press in case of maternity'. Alternatively, he could have opted for rubbing noses, or sitting on the Garden of Eden piano stool (the majority of pregnant young wives at my last church swore the coffee lounge music seat had something to do with it).

Thank God his birds-and-bees research gave him a more ingenious brainwave. And if he amazed himself with the final design, his creatures were even more astounded.

This gift reveals the Giver as does no other. He has a sense of humour, that's for sure. And more. He has a sense of beauty, oneness, warmth, mystery, fun, delight, intimacy . . . . The words are endless.

So, sadly, is our misuse of what they describe.

Shame that we employ such a gift for our own profit. Our forebears abused it with sacred prostitutes in a futile bid for rain. Some today use it as if going to the toilet; simply to relieve a need. Others sell it for money, advance or power in a relationship. Of course, those who do so miss the whole point. Sex is the last great amateur art.

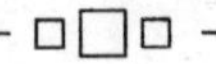

What do you do about a hell on earth? What do you do when you know that the residents are heading for an eternal hell that is much worse? And not only them. So too is the rest of humanity for all of history.

What do you do when you are God? What do you do when to do nothing would make you the very devil himself! An accessory. An accomplice. A bystander who shrugs while thugs thrive.

The wrath of God

God totally hates sin. This violent reaction against evil is necessary because he is holy. Holiness and sin go together like leeches and cream.

We human beings are often unhappy about choosing between extremes. Certainly, we don't like the devil, but equally we shy away from heavenly haloes.

Naturally, we much prefer the happy medium. We'd be content with a sort of in-between god who turns a blind eye to our personal little human frailties. If only he could overlook our overeating, the illegal 'freebies' at work and the extramarital sex.

Sometimes we go to extraordinary lengths to accommodate even our most outrageous appetites. After all, it's very hard living up to this holy God who cannot abide our sin.

New Testament writer Paul says that we are 'by nature objects of wrath' (Eph 2:3). But he goes on to point out that God also wasn't happy exercising his wrath on sin, because he still loved the sinner. So he, in Christ, became the 'deliverer' from the wrath to come (1 Thess 1:10). '. . . God demonstrates his own love for us in this: While we were still sinners, Christ died for us' (Rom 5:8).

If you're not in a crowded bus or train while reading this, feel quite free to add a loud 'Hallelujah' at this point.

A God of love had no alternative but to purge the whole land. Divine ethnic cleansing. Joshua knew this already. He had long before received his orders via Moses:

> In the cities of the nations the Lord your God is giving you as an inheritance, do not leave alive anything that breathes. Completely destroy them – the Hittites, Amorites, Canaanites, Perizzites, Hivites and Jebusites – as the Lord your God has commanded you. Otherwise, they will teach you to follow all the detestable things they do in worshipping their gods, and you will sin against the Lord your God (Deut 20:16–18).

The Hittites

. . . a warring people whose empire stretched from the Black Sea down into Israel. Abraham bought from them an area around Hebron. By Joshua's day they were in decline, commanding only the central ridge below Jerusalem.

The Amorites

. . . a catch-all name for those in Canaan, but the pure Amorites commanded the hill regions either side of the Jordan. At one time they were described as 'being unacquainted with civilised life'.

The poets were to declare Joshua's coming defeat of Amorite kings Sihon and Og as his greatest moments (Ps 135:11). See also in Chapter 12 'A lot to confess'.

The Canaanites

. . . believed to come from the son of Ham, Canaan, who was cursed by God for dishonouring his father, Noah (Gen 9). From Canaan's son originated all the other neighbouring 'ites'.

The Jebusites

. . . descended from Japheth, third son of Noah. They were hill dwellers around Jerusalem, which they called Jebus. A Jebusite was a dweller of that city.

The Hivites and the Perizzites

The Hivites were from the loins of Canaan. The origins of the others are uncertain. Both peoples lived in the north-west area called Lebanon. Some had also settled inland at Shechem and in the Judean hills. Together with nearby tribes, they could muster 'a huge army, as numerous as the sand on the seashore' (Josh 11:4).

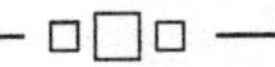

This land of Canaan was the crossroads of the world. Anybody who was anybody used it with their camel trains and armies. This was Caanan Junction, the Clapham or Crewe of the Middle East.

'Welcome to hell on earth,' the border signpost might have read.

Joshua knew it. And more. He knew that God had a dream to rewrite the destination on that signpost. He wanted to point the human race back to himself.

This was to be a replay of the Garden of Eden against an international backdrop. Here, the world would see enacted a beautiful loving relationship between Israel and himself. The purpose of this living drama, played out at the busiest intersection of life, was to show a lost world the road out of hell and into heaven.

Here, we move through and beyond the wrath of God to that great romance at the heart of the universe and of history. The people of the world were the guests at a marriage really made in heaven. The bridegroom was God and the bride was

Israel. And Joshua found himself in the privileged position of being, along with Moses, the matchmaker.

Mills and Boon has nothing on this. Barbara Cartland, eat your heart out. This is pure poetry in the motion of history, and it began with God rescuing his bride from Egypt and her fate of living death.

Israel, God's bride

God's people were inspired to see their relationship in terms of a marriage, as they looked back on their courtship with him.

The Lord would call Israel back as if she were his wife, Isaiah wrote (54:6), and Hosea reported God as saying that his people 'will call me "my husband"' (2:16).

The Song of Songs could also be seen in the same light. This beautiful oriental poem illuminates the holy intimacy between God and his people.

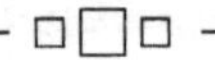

He swept his betrothed across the sea to a marriage on his holy mountain. At Sinai, they exchanged vows. He promised to love, comfort, honour and keep her. She vowed to love, cherish and to obey. They had just finished an extended honeymoon touring in the wilderness – longer than intended. His bride had an attack of nerves when it came to settling into her new home. But now they had come to an understanding, and, at long last, he planned to carry his bride across the threshold of the River Jordan and into the homeland he had promised to her.

Meanwhile, Joshua stood on the banks, still wondering how he would manage minus Moses and that miraculous staff.

5
Secrets of Success

'Go over and possess the land.'

That's the motto of the Northern Evangelical Trust.[1] *NET was born in 1985 after Brian Jackson felt God calling him to leave a highly paid transport manager's job in Accrington, Lancashire, and help inspire northern churches to evangelise. NET has subsequently helped local churches to win thousands for Christ.*

It now has four full-time workers with their families, a fifteen-strong team of one-year workers, two residential centres, a bookshop, café and resource centre, a 60ft canal barge, a double-deck coffee and outreach bus and a 500-seater mission tent. Annually, NET involves hundreds of youth in evangelistic camps and events. Brian is still urging them on into their modern Canaan to win more people for the Lord.

Why? Because he heard God promise, 'I will be with you.'

His cousin, Dave Shore, worked alongside him until taking time out for an MA. As a youth himself, Dave's main purpose in life was to make sure the police in Darwen, Lancashire, never had a moment's peace. With a little more effort, he could have had his own personal crime figures. Then God took over.

Dave was so astounded with the good news that Jesus

had saved him that he devoted every waking moment to telling others. Anywhere! Even Tanzania, where he joined Manchester evangelist Paul Morley.

They were inspired to help relieve the poverty they encountered, especially the plight of abandoned and abused children.

Bethany was the solution – a thirty-acre complex on the shores of Lake Victoria.[2] *It now provides 7,000 gallons of purified water for the area's villages each day, treats hundreds each month at its daily clinics, runs its custom-built units on solar heating panels and brings starving orphans off the wild streets of Mwanza in a specially adapted Land Rover and trailer. Once at Bethany, the kids settle into their new family, a Christian community of British and Tanzanian volunteers.*

It has taken eight years. They did it because they knew God would be with them.

* * *

Modern-day Joshuas both.

But if the original Joshua had not done his job so well, today's stories might never have been.

'Go!' said the Lord. And Joshua went. Nervously. With tiny steps of faltering courage and with hardly any strength. He doubted if anything could happen when there were no tricks and no Moses. It's the identical feeling to that of the budding youth leader quaking before teeny terrors. The housewife knows it in the supermarket on meeting a friend who desperately needs some guidance. So does the leader of an 'over-our-dead-body' church.

'Be strong and courageous,' the Lord said to Joshua (Josh 1:6). And to us. 'Do not be terrified; do not be discouraged. No one will be able to stand against you all the days of your life' (Josh 1:9, 5).

Strong sounds. Comforting, reassuring sentences. But the

words Joshua was really waiting for were the same words that grab all God's warriors in any age: 'As I was with Moses, so I will be with you; I will never leave you nor forsake you' (Josh 1:5).

With such words you can take on the world. You can battle through the gates of hell on your patch. You can face a Jordan of any description. You could even write a Christian book. We, like Joshua, can go forth because we know the golden secret of fighting on the Lord's side.

Victory secret

'God's workers do not work up towards victory. They work down from it.' That was the inspired conclusion of the great preacher and writer Alan Redpath in his book on Joshua.[3] He explained that God's modern-day followers 'do not struggle towards victory, but we stand in it because of the Cross and an empty tomb'.

Not, of course, that Joshua's foundations were so firm. His confidence was founded only on what God had done through Moses, the staff of Aaron, a few plagues and an empty Exodus sea. These were added to a few hand-me-down stories about great, great, great whatever Abraham and co. And on this and little else he was prepared to go over and possess the land. On so little!

How much more should we do, knowing so much more of God and his might?

The Book of success

Joshua had a second secret strategy that guaranteed success – the Book! Actually, it was a few scrolls of soft animal hide. On them Moses, with no doubt more than a little help from his chief assistant, had set out God's recipe for victory in the whole of life. This was the makings of the first five books of our Bible. 'Do not let this Book of the Law depart from your mouth; meditate on it day and night, so that you may be careful to do everything written in it. Then you will be prosperous and successful' (Josh 1:8).

Mystery writers or Moses?

Just who held the quill reeds that penned the first five books of the Old Testament (the Pentateuch)?

Up to 250 years ago there was only one answer: Moses (with Joshua adding his boss's obituary – Deuteronomy 34:5–12). Since then, there have been more learned speculations than letters in this present sentence.

Ezra, the one who rediscovered the Book of the Law, was once odds-on favourite. Learned hunches involving mystery scribes went in and out of fashion. Tips about one editor gathering many fragments of text enjoyed short odds before dropping out of the running. Some texts addressed God as 'Elohim' while others seemed to prefer 'Yahweh'. Maybe there were two writers. But what about the part when God became Elohim-Yahweh? A third unknown scribe?

Then perhaps the priests added their Leviticus bits. And surely Deuteronomy came from a separate legal source. Others around the time of Charles Darwin suggested that the Old Testament evolved and grew like Topsy.

There is a whole raft of arguments for and against all the above, and *The New Bible Dictionary* (IVP) deals with them well if you want to study the form.

It must be said that learned scholars have unearthed many useful tips, immensely improving our understanding and interpretation of the texts. However, it has to be admitted that most of their fancies fell at early fences.

These were sometimes backed by scholars who unfairly handicapped themselves. They believed that the Bible was just another human book, and should be criticised as such. God's involvement was minimised, almost to non-runner status. Suffice to conclude that their success was rather less than that of the average tabloid race tipster.

When God told Joshua to meditate on the Book of the Law night and day, it must already have been substantial. It must have been sufficient to guide and direct his people in a new land in a new age. Large tracks of the books claim to be the work of Moses (e.g., Exodus 20–23; 34; Deuteronomy 5–26; 31).

However, it is more than probable that the full writings of the period were assembled in the form we now have them around the seventh century BC.

With regard to events before Moses, he probably collected together, under God's guidance, the various stories which had been passed down the generations. Oral tradition, it's called. The Jews were pastmasters at passing on accurate and precise details of just how God had worked in the past. Mainly because their almighty God ordered them to do it.

God's word, as we now have it, is his sixty-six-book library of life; his manual to achieve success.

Instructions and my brain don't always go together. A great DIY man I'll never be. I even struggled to qualify for MFI. Remember the do-it-yourself furniture? Despite picture-book guides, I was always left sifting debris for the missing screw, or screaming red-faced at innocent, left-over panels. God has used this aspect of modern life to develop my character. My screams are now hardly audible in the next street.

So many of us have chunks of our lives strewn about our feet, uncertain as to how they fit into God's plan. We have his instruction Book, but do we read it? Do we meditate on it day and night?

Murphy's Law dictates that if something can go wrong, it will. My version decrees that the nearer you live to the speed of sound, the quicker things will disintegrate into chaos. Life's too mad to walk, don't you find? It's too frantic to fully read the instructions, let alone meditate on them day and night. We consequently end up screaming in pain when the furniture of our life begins to fall apart. One day, I keep telling myself, it will sink in that speed-reading is simply a faster way to failure.

Casual glances, and especially a once-a-week public reading of the instruction Book, are a one hundred per cent guarantee that I will not prosper nor have success in the Lord.

Prosperity and success

'The Lord is my banker, my credit is good. He maketh me to lie down in the consciousness of omnipresent abundance. He giveth me the key to his strongbox. He restoreth my faith in his riches; He guideth in the paths of prosperity for His name's sake.'

Thus began Charles Fillmore's prosperity gospel just before the turn of the century in America. It has rippled down the generations in various forms ever since.

This is, of course, not what God was promising those who meditate on his word night and day.

He had in mind our spiritual success. He wanted us to be centred on his spiritual wealth. He yearns to pour riches upon us from heaven. The last thing he wanted us to be was centred on self and the riches of earth (Phil 4:11–13, 19).

'Seek ye first the kingdom of God,' was how he put it.

This is so important that God begins his message to Joshua with it. Of all the things in life God could have chosen to highlight, he picks this one.

'Read my book,' he commands.

As this is so important, let me risk another picture.

My research for this book ended in Jerusalem. I had half a day to kill before my flight home, and I found myself at the Yad Vashem holocaust museum. Even now, as I remember, my throat tightens and my eyes water. Once again, I'm enveloped in blackness, save for a million starlights. They twinkle in the many-mirrored hall of remembrance to the one and a half million children who died in the death camps. The account of one Jewish concentration camp writer still echoes:

> The noise of an engine woke me, and I looked out as a covered wagon reversed to a ditch beside the window of our hut. Slowly, the back began to tip and its load tumbled out, almost without sound. In the fading light, I assumed it was rubbish. But why so little noise? Two figures climbed from the cab with shovels and began to fill in the ditch. Only then did my eyes grow accustomed to twilight. The ditch was full of dead babies.

I cried in the hall of remembrance that day. It was for the children. But there was something else. Possibly, it was a fresh vision of why there had to be a Holy Land. The salvation story experiences of the previous days swam into fine focus. I wept over Jerusalem, over the state of the world and my part in it. Yet, there was still something more.

It was on the plane home when a full mental picture emerged from the sadness. It was of gaunt-eyed skeletons shuffling through the gates of Auschwitz. We've all seen the pictures. They couldn't take the food offered by the rescuing allies. Chocolate was left untouched. It was just too rich for them. Into this picture, other people walked. It was us – the 'us' being Western Christians. I was crying for myself and my church. So many of us limping, listless and languid. Spiritual skeletons; undernourished and thin. Christians who hardly fed themselves on God's word. Just like those in Corinth city in St Paul's day.

'I gave you milk,' Paul wrote to them, 'not solid food, for you were not ready for it. Indeed, you are still not ready. You are still worldly' (1 Cor 3:2–3).

'You're still little babes,' he was crying, 'still sucking milk. I wanted to give you meat but you've never grown up.'

He could have been writing about us. The sirloin steak of Scripture is untouched. The wraith-like figures in my picture hobbled through their wildernesses on rake-thin legs. They shuddered by their personal Jordans – unable, or unwilling, to cross. Some camped in their deserts scared of fighting or advancing. They waited for a peace that was impossible without victory. Still others, fearful of trusting God, waited for a pleasure cruiser before crossing. Saddest of all were those who had made Canaan's banks, only to remain on board. Fear of disembarking had turned their cruiser into a prison ship.

Canaan = life

There's a problem in our ancient hymns.

The Jordan equals 'death of deaths', we are told. 'Landed safe on Canaan's side' equals arrival in heaven.[4] Carry me through death to heaven.

But the Bible begs to differ. The writing on the poetic licence of hymn writers is smudged.

The river, according to Joshua, represents that which keeps us from all that God wants to give to us. It is all those things that leave us wandering in our wilderness of sin.

Canaan is not an escape into heaven. It is entry into the peace and warfare of walking God's way.

Now this really is something to sing about. That thing that keeps you from God right at this moment can be swept aside and miraculously walled-up. Our great

Jehovah can guide you through it. And he will be with you, just as he was with Moses and Joshua.

On the other side is the promised life.

New settlers welcome.

Yes, I cried for the death camp children. And the tears came because we could have prevented their deaths. If only we had followed God's word more accurately through the centuries . . . . If only we had meditated on it night and day . . . . If only . . . .

A whole war might have been avoided. Millions may have been saved. And those one and a half million children would not have needed a hall of remembrance (see panel below for further explanation).

This down-to-earth practical Book is not just for our 'quiet times'. It provides more than my personal prosperity. It's about world peace and security. It's about saving babies.

- The Book that could have saved millions -

The Holocaust and even World War II might arguably have been prevented by sound scriptural teaching.

It simply needed German Christians to read and understand their Bibles, and then for them to check their leaders and their ideas against it.

Pastor and theologian Dietrich Bonhoeffer warned of the Nazification of his church in 1933. He helped draft the Barmen Declaration which rejected the infamous Aryan principles that sent millions of Jews to the gas chambers. German Christians (*Deutsche Christen*), on the other hand, even went as far as disowning the Old Testament and the Jewish foundations of Christianity.

Of course, the Nazis should not take all the blame for

war atrocities. The roots were planted when primitive Christian Europe branded Jews as the 'Christ killer', failing to understand Scripture's emphasis on the guilt of all humanity at the foot of the cross.

Adolf Hitler had such a warped view of what God was saying in his Bible. He wrote in *Mein Kampf*:

> Should the Jew . . . triumph over the people of this world, his crown will be the funeral wreath of mankind . . . And so I believe today that my conduct is in accordance with the will of the Almighty creator. In standing guard against the Jew I am defending the handiwork of the Lord.[5]

Hitler would have been better reading his Bible than writing *Mein Kampf*.

And, of course, he's not the only guilty one. You and I know that the times we fail to light our paths with the searchlight of God's truth are exactly those times we stumble.

The writer of Psalm 119 knew this too.

'I will obey your decrees' (v 8).

'I have chosen the way of truth' (v 30).

'The unfolding of your words gives light' (v 130).

'I obey your statutes, for I love them greatly' (v 167).

You can't imagine the psalmist who wrote, 'Your word is a lamp to my feet' (v 105) starting a world war and killing one and a half million people, can you?

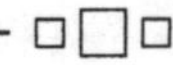

Talking and relating

A third secret that propelled Joshua to Jordan's banks was a new relationship. Something was happening between God and himself. The 'I'll be with you' promise had sealed it.

'How can you believe God will give us the Promised Land?' many river-watchers might have nervously asked.

'I don't have to believe,' he could answer. 'Now, I know!'

Personal experience of this God brought certainty. He had discovered the amazing truth: to open up to God is to find God's arms already wide open in welcome. In personal experience of God, a personal living relationship was born.

'Get your supplies ready,' was Joshua's full and confident reply. 'Three days from now you will cross the Jordan here to go in and take possession of the land the Lord your God is giving you for your own' (Josh 1:11).

Eighty-five per cent of the population say they believe in God in one form or another. They have an 'I–it' relationship – the 'it' being whatever 'it' is out there. Of course, even some church people have this variety of religious relationship. Not all, by any means, have broken through to the 'I–thou' relationship.

This occurs when two people connect, talk, share and mutually care for, and about, each other. This is Joshua telling God that he is scared witless. This is God coming in the quietness of the desert night to give him courage and strength. This is you and I, when faced with the insurmountable, begging for divine mountaineering skills. This is God taking us in those everlasting arms and whispering, 'It's okay, my child. I've got hold of you. Now, lift your left foot into that crevice and bring your right hand up to that outcrop . . . . I will be with you as I was with Moses, as I was with Joshua, as I am with everybody else who works for me.'

And this is life. Real life. So says the One who is the New Testament Joshua and much more besides – the Lord Jesus Christ: 'Now this is eternal life: that they [my followers] may know you, the only true God, and Jesus Christ, whom you have sent' (Jn 17:3).

Joshua was getting to know God for himself. Not through Nun and Mum. Not second hand through escorting his boss on his divine mission. This was Joshua and God. Communicating. Being real with each other. Praying.

There are books on prayer and books of prayers. There are volumes on what form the prayers should take. Rubrics in italics tell us who should say them, in what physical position, at which geographical location and how many times. We love reading about prayer. Christian bookshop sales tell us. It's the doing that's the problem. We'd be super Christians if we prayed as much as we read about praying. No. I mean really prayed; really connected with the Lord.

And Joshua did it.

He talked, and then he listened and listened and listened. That's why he and Israel got so far. We talk and talk and then talk some more and go round in circles. So, we read and read and only travel across a page. When talking and reading fail, we fake motion by jumping on to man-made movements.

'What the Church needs today,' wrote E. M. Bounds in his classic *Power through Prayer*, 'is not more machinery or better, not new organisations or more novel methods, but men whom the Holy Ghost can use – men of prayer, men mighty in prayer.'

Prayer makes the man and the woman. Prayer makes the children's worker, the church leader, the preacher. Prayer makes the church go round, and it made Joshua the great success he is now undoubtedly on his way to being.

Throw away the books. Even this one.

Pray!

Really! Pray!

You're still reading!

Go on. It'll only take a lifetime.

See. I'll stop writing while we do it . . . .

Okay. So I cheated. Our difficulty is knowing that nobody will stop for us to pray. We have to do the stopping.

You need to sing 'I did it God's way'

Standing in victory. Going by the Book. Divinely relating. A fourth secret ensured success for Joshua. He used the head God gave him, but he placed God ahead of it.

'God helps those who help themselves,' many glibly trot out. It's a myth. Not true, not for a minute.

Yes, God certainly expects us to do our bit. And no, we're not supposed to sit on the banks of life waiting for God to build a cross-channel tunnel under our Jordans. But there is true spiritual balance, and Joshua got it just right.

If Joshua had lived and died in our day, we could be certain of one thing: Frank Sinatra's *My Way* would not be played at the crematorium. The Hebrew chorus would revamp it and raise the roof with, 'He did it God's way!'

Certainly, God expects us to help ourselves, but only under his directions. Joshua grasped this.

On getting his marching orders, he did not rush off and do his own thing. First, he got the officers to tell the people to get ready. It was a direct order from God (Josh 1:10). Second, he took directions from God when two and a half tribes wanted to stay on the wrong side of the Jordan. He remembered what had been written in the Book of the Law that allowed the tribes of Reuben, Gad and half of Manasseh to settle on the east bank (Num 32).

A hothead general might have court-martialled the lot of them; sent them white feathers; told them they were a bunch of cowards. The reverse was in fact the case. The two and a half tribes knew what justice demanded. They knew that, though their families and flocks remained, they should fight alongside their brothers. They even insisted that they should lead the way into battle. Joshua accepted the justice and the tribes reinforced their support: 'Whatever you have commanded us we will do, and wherever you send us we will go. Just as we fully obeyed Moses, so we will obey you. Only may the Lord your God be with you as he was with Moses' (Josh 1:16–17).

They were soon to discover whether or not he was.

Cults and sects

Joshua has a few lessons for the thousand and one cults and sects in modern Britain. Overly-dictatorial churches might also learn.

Joshua observed the golden rule that governs all human/divine relationship – freedom of choice. The two and a half tribes that wanted to settle east of Jordan were allowed to make their own bed, wherever they chose.

A group I serve with researched the horrific cult scene of nineties Britain.[6] We identified the controls that imprison thousands in wills other than their own.

Mind-control techniques include hypnosis, chanting, peer pressure, love-bombing, finger-pointing, subliminal messages, time-sense deprivation, verbal abuse, sleep deprivation, guilt and fear.

There was:

Dictatorial leadership with rigid rules.

Denial of privileges for disobedience.

Deprivation of privacy, personal choice and food.

Defamation of those outside the cult, especially members' families.

Disintegration of will.

Distortion of biblical teaching.

On a personal note, I was struck by the number of Christian churches involved in denial of free will. Their principles were perfect and biblical. Their practices were cultic and definitely unbiblical.

Notes

[1] The Northern Evangelical Trust, Abbey Book and Resource Centre, 188–190 Union Road, Oswaldtwistle, Accrington, Lancs.

[2] The Bethany Project, Co-ordinator Graham Pountain (01254 876884 or 822767 and Personnel Jo Hartley (01254 670145).

[3] Alan Redpath, *Victorious Christian Living* (Pickering and English).

[4] 'Guide me, O Thou great Jehovah.' William Williams (1717–1791).

[5] Adolf Hitler, *Mein Kampf*, vol 1 (London 1939), p 66.

[6] Evangelical Alliance Coalition on the Occult and New Spiritualities. *Twisted Truth*, the title of their helpful research leaflet, is available from the Evangelical Alliance.

6

Myth or Miracle?

The smile on his face was patient. He was doing his best to be kind. His voice was slow and gentle, pitched precisely right to deal with a naive junior-aged child who still believed that Adam and Eve were real people. I ran an uneasy finger round the inside of my dog collar and tried to look what I was – fiftysomething.

'You see,' and I half expected my clergy colleague to add 'my poor child' as he leaned across the coffee table towards me at the diocesan conference, 'let's get back to Bultmann and his idea of myth. Certainly, there's truth in the Garden of Eden story – '

One of my eyebrows did a Mexican wave at this point, and my protagonist's hands shot up to quell any rebellious query I might have.

'Oh, yessss!' he stressed. 'Believe me. I mean it. Truth! But, you see, it all depends on what you mean by truth, and what's more . . . .'

My eyebrow had probably risen more in hopeless resignation. I'd had a hundred such debates with similar liberals and had always found them to be rather narrow-minded and fundamentalist for my tastes.

'There's nothing quite so illiberal as a liberal,' a bishop

once said to me. Their minds can only stretch as far as their experience, and their fundamental bottom line appears to be something like, 'God's not a magician. He doesn't suddenly invent human beings from clay and spare ribs, or change water into wine, or wall up oceans and rivers to save his people getting their feet wet. These are all myths. They contain truth but are not necessarily themselves true.'

So, what are we to make of Joshua?

He's not only got to get three million across a river that thinks it's a lake, we're also going to read that he blew down Jericho's walls with trumpets and made the sun stand still for nearly a day (Josh 6; 10).

And further: Joshua never reads like a fabricated tale. It's more *News at Ten* than *Bedtime Story*. See what I mean:

> Consecrate yourselves, for tomorrow the Lord will do amazing things among you . . . as soon as the priests who carry the ark of the Lord – the Lord of all the earth – set foot in the Jordan, its waters flowing downstream will be cut off and stand up in a heap (Josh 3:5, 13).

This is the language of fact rather than fable. These are the words of somebody who actually believes in miracles. And with this, we are almost at the point of uncovering the fifth of our man's secrets. It's all about letting God be God.

It will become clearer as we unravel this conflict between the modern mind and ancient events. But allow me a little dramatic licence and let's take the argument back to Joshua's day in a bid to understand it.

This, with apologies to Beckett, is a sort of *Waiting for Godot*, in the style of yesterday.

ACT ONE

[Note to casting: I want Harrison Ford to play Joshua, with a Hebrew version of his Indiana Jones. For Eli, get me Ron

Moody recreating his Fagin role in Oliver Twist, *which he then needs to blend with the Artful Dodger.]*

SCENE ONE (AND ONLY)

A warm April evening. A tent. Off stage, the drone of distant rushing water blending with the subdued excitement of a crowd. Joshua half sits, half leans against a steep sand-dune. He struggles with a knot in his sandal lace before turning in for the night.

Enter ELI, *a headstrong young priest, one of those detailed to carry the ark of the covenant into the Jordan flood waters.*

ELI [*hands held aloft with a shrug of apology*]: So. Big day tomorrow. Early start, eh? That you should have so many headaches! Ssssh!

JOSHUA [*guessing he now had another*]: You want I should give you an appointment, my holy friend?

ELI: So formal? [*Pause, as if to reflect on best diplomatic way a thirty-year-old can criticise his elderly leader.*] Erm . . . this ark, Joshua. [*Forefinger begins to wag.*] A dangerous lark. They're not going to understand. You should not be so flippant . . . and we priests are going to be underneath it.

JOSHUA [*still picking at the stubborn knot*]: You have a point?

ELI [*slightly irritated*]: Point!smoint! You think a raging torrent should sit up and obey the moment we priests dip our toes in. Hah!

JOSHUA: Cold feet?

ELI: Cold logic. [*Stony faced.*] Cool mind!

JOSHUA [*smiling up at* ELI]: Is not the hand of God bigger than your head?

ELI [*exploding*]: Look! You've done a good job. So far, so good. And I'm the first to defend you whenever they start on about you. You've fed us, you've watered –

JOSHUA [*quietly*]: Not I. Where on earth am I going to find heavenly food day and night in the desert for nigh on forty years – ?

ELI: See! There you go again. It's food, Joshua. Just normal everyday, mundane, earthly produce! It grows. It happens. It comes every morning because it comes every morning. That's it. End of story. That's life! Listen, my friend [*in unfriendly tones.*] take care that you don't lose what we've gained. They'll take so much of this miracle talk and then . . . . [*He halts, unwilling to put the rest into words. Pause. He thaws, rubs his hands as though washing and smiles slyly.*] Looook! Sure, we'll keep the gullible, the poor, the uneducated. No problem. But what will it profit to gain the whole unwashed world if we lose the real soul of our economy? You'll lose the good thinkers. And the traders. They need to plan. Business is business. This amazing God talk is not good for it. Let's not spoil it. A few weeks, the harvest floods will drain away, and then we can ford the river. No problem. [*An ingratiating grin widens.*] What do you say, my leader?

JOSHUA [*still struggling with his sandals*]: This knot is one of the worst I've had.

ELI: Never mind the laces!

JOSHUA [*sadly*]: It will have to be cut out.

ELI: Forget the sandals!

JOSHUA: I have.

ELI: Then what are we talking about?

JOSHUA: You. [*Slight pause while priest recovers.*]

ELI [*blustering*]: Cut me out!? [*Recovering quickly.*] Mark this well, Joshua. We've had your tales of seas parting right up to here. [*He taps forehead with the edge of his flat hand.*] Your stories of miraculous staffs, and divine plagues and heavenly food are, well, just that. Stories!

JOSHUA: I was there.

ELI: It was forty years ago, for heaven's sake, man! You've been wandering in the desert, and in this god-forsaken wilderness, who knows, our minds do as well. [*Becoming kinder.*] We're none of us getting any younger. Face it, Joshua. They're stories. 'Course they have value for us. Great inspiration. Good moral lessons. But that's it. They're myths. It doesn't matter whether they happened or not. What matters is the moral truth behind the story. Get too literal and you spoil it for everybody. People these days are just not into this miracle business.

JOSHUA [*pause for long, hard look at* ELI, *who grows more uncomfortable*]: Thirty years old yet, Eli, and you were there to see the plagues of forty years ago? You think you know better than those who wrote it down. You're bigger than Moses? More educated? Perhaps more sophisticated? Tell me, Eli, why should we believe you more than those who recorded it all as history? As fact?

ELI: But we've never experienced seas and rivers heaping up.

JOSHUA: So, all of a sudden your experience is God?

ELI: Our minds can't take it in.

JOSHUA: Who needs a god as small as your mind?

ELI: You demand the impossible.

JOSHUA: Look. The Book of the Law is full of miracles –

ELI [*scoffing*]: Like eighty-year-old Sarah getting pregnant and – .

JOSHUA [*smiling*]: You want I should ask God to do the same for you, eh, Eli?

ELI: And another thing. You helped Moses put it together. Why include all these miracles in the first place?

JOSHUA: Without them, we'd just have our story and not his story. Leave out God's acts and we could fit the rest on the backside of a kid goat's hide! And where would be the inspiration in that? In man's puny acts? We might as well read the hieroglyphics of Pharaoh Tut or my Aunt Rachel's tent wall graffiti!

* * *

And now back to prose.

We can now spell out Joshua's fifth secret of success. He recognised the obvious: God has to be bigger than our heads. Anything smaller wouldn't be worth worshipping.

Man should certainly seek to know God but stop short of being a know-all. It is easier for an ocean to fit into a desert gnat's eyeglass than for a poor man to squeeze all of God into his tiny brain. The normal human being – I mean the thinking, rational variety – should expect one thing if he attempts this exercise. There'll be a lot left over that he won't understand. Let him once claim to have grasped God with his intellect, and one of two things will have happened. He'll have died and gone to face the real God in heaven, or he'll be alive and face-to-face with a false god made in his own image.

Christian writer and teacher David Pawson tackles this myth-or-miracle area superbly in his tapes on Joshua, and concludes:

> Joshua presents us with real people in real places. You can go and see the Jordan River. I've baptised people in it. Jericho's a real place – I've stood on the ruins of it. The Canaanites were real people. Archaeology demonstrates that. The Israelites are real people; their descendants are still with us. Furthermore, the Book of Joshua claims to be written by eye-witnesses. It's written in the first person plural – 'We marched around the walls of Jericho.' Now that's a direct claim of people who were there.
>
> Why should it be thought that a scholar in the twentieth century AD knows better what happened than somebody who was actually there? It's a strange prejudice that comes to such a conclusion. So, the book claims to be a record of events written at the time, and one of the frequent little phrases that comes in the book is 'and it is there to this day', so the first readers could go and check up on what had been recorded.
>
> Now, to dismiss all this as myth is a very arrogant thing to do.[1]

I visited the site of many miracles as many do on their Holy Land tours. There is strong evidence for these miracles today.

The profoundest moment in preparing this book was to stand on the excavated mounds of Tell Jericho,[2] the oldest recorded city in the world.

The tell, a hill no bigger than a football stadium, had witnessed hundreds of dramas in dozens of generations, and I could see for myself the civilisations, thinly layered, in trenches made by Professor John Garstang and later by Dame Kathleen Kenyon.

New interpretations of the evidence at Jericho and many

other ancient sites now indicate that for two generations the sophisticated Canaanite lifestyle collapsed and was taken over by a simpler, less-developed culture. And the band of ex-slaves-cum-nomads that was Israel certainly fits that description. This phenomenon can also be seen in other cities destroyed by the Israelites, such as Lachish.

Detectives of the past

Bible-believers have at times been embarrassed by archaeology. In the thirties, John Garstang's digs claimed to lay bare the fallen walls of Jericho. Twenty years later, Kathleen Kenyon's trenches showed that Garstang had failed to account for surface erosion and that he was consequently looking at the wrong level.

Dame Kathleen reluctantly concluded that if Joshua did reach Jericho around 1240 BC, as tradition insisted, then he had problems. At that time there were no walls and nobody living in Jericho.

Archaeologists are gifted detectives, sifting evidence before prosecuting their case. But, just as real detectives have the Guildford Four and Birmingham Six, so archaeologists too have their errors.

Newly unearthed archaeological evidence, based on a new chronology of Egyptian Pharaohs and other issues, indicates that Joshua and the Exodus was around 1440 BC, or even earlier.[3]

On re-examining Jericho's trenches for that period, leading Egyptologist and historian Dr David Rohl concluded: 'Biblical Jericho, destroyed by Joshua's forces, is to be identified with the Middle Bronze Age city at Tell es-Sultan [old Jericho] which was devastated by fire and remained a desolate ruin for several centuries thereafter.'[4]

The River Jordan is already shrinking in Joshua's eyes.

First, he learns that he does not have to swim against the tide for victory. In God, he's already an Olympic champion. He has the victory. Second, he's got the Maker's instructions on how to overcome life itself. Third, he knows the Author intimately and has power through prayer. Fourth, he can hum 'I did it God's way' and mean it.

Next, he lets God be God – bigger than his brains, greater than nature; a God before whom a swollen, raging torrent was merely a trickle.

Of course, he still had to act on it all, and that was Joshua's sixth secret of success.

Notes

[1] David Pawson Teaching Ministry, Anchor Recordings, 72 The Street, Kennington, Ashford, Kent TN24 9HS.

[2] Known as Tell-es-Sultan.

[3] David Rohl, *A Test of Time (The Bible – from Myth to History)* (Arrow).

[4] *Ibid*, Conclusion 29, p 305.

7
Moving God's People

Hoshea made a new noun for himself by being a verb. He was a doer. And God can always use doers. Joshua was a dynamic being who made things happen at every level he reached.

This Action Man trait was obvious from the start. It must have been for Moses to have enlisted him. It was further shaped as the backroom boffin behind the Exodus campaign. As Moses' chief assistant, Joshua must literally have held together the great man and his mission until relief came with the founding of the Hebrew civil service (see panel).

Joshua then advanced to James Bond status, 005 in the list of spies sent behind enemy lines in Canaan (Num 13:8). The Amalekite campaign brought promotion to field marshal.

Now, on the banks of the Jordan, his divine career has peaked as the top five-star general over allied tribal forces of more than half a million (Ex 17:8–15; Num 2:32).

Hebrew civil service

Joshua and his boss were heading for the uncivil service which comes from sheer exhaustion. Then Moses' father-in-law, Jethro, rode in to camp on a family outing (Ex 18).

Jethro quickly noted early signs of burnout. As a priest and leader himself, he knew that even God's heroes could only take so much. He was horrified at Moses' one-man-band act before an audience of three million Israelites.

'Why do you alone sit as judge, while all these people stand round you . . . ?' Jethro asked. ' . . . you will only wear yourselves out . . . I will give you some advice. . . .'

Moses had cast himself in the macho Charlton Heston role while Hollywood was still jungle. Jethro advised him to drop the superman disguise and stop trying to be the servant of all.

A civil service of helpers was needed.

'Select capable men,' said his father-in-law, ' . . . and appoint them as officials over thousands, hundreds, fifties and tens . . . . That will make your load lighter. . . .' (See leadership roles in Chapter 11.)

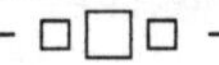

Such a towering hero, I ask you! What's to become of us mere mortals? To use a basic Hebrewism – and the Hebrews could be very basic – our profile of Joshua can produce either inspiration or constipation!

'Wow! What a meteoric slave-to-saviour rise! Could be me, God willing!'

Or, 'No way, Hoshea! God forbid!'

One moves us, and we don't need words to describe what the other does for us. Suffice to say that the insecure 'poor-little-old-me' syndrome peeps from behind our fragile façade of self-esteem and refuses to budge.

What we need to see at this moment is that Joshua's rise is just not natural. It's supernatural (plus a pinch of the natural)!

He is a beautiful example of God's golden spiritual principle: God gives a little. We use well. God gives more (Lk 12:35–48).

God is not after overnight superheroes. He doesn't want instant generals. He doesn't demand Einstein brains nor Joshua talent. He simply wants characters full of his charisma – loyal servants who will make themselves available for his use. Let us remember: Joshua was a cadet for forty years. He was an aide-de-camp for another forty before the five stars were eventually pinned on him. Eighty years' basic training!

God knows that we only move by taking steps, and Olympic triple-jumpers we may never be! God asks us, and empowers us, to walk in his footsteps. The length between them is tailor-made for each of us. No more. No less. Nothing to fear.

When I was a child, my dad let me stand on his feet while he walked. He even held my hands to keep me balanced. If you're smiling now, you'll have done the same with your dad or your kids. Our heavenly Father loves playing the same game with us.

So be inspired. This, after all, is why this divine drama is played out before us in the Old Testament. Let's take our seats and watch, so that we too might be moved to action. See what propels our character, that we too might aspire to be God's heroes . . . that we might play our parts.

Act One always comes before Act Two

Obvious, really. So you would think. But not among the 'actors' of the religious stage. These not only get their acts mixed up. They lose the plot. I know. Following my world debut, I did this for twenty-eight years.

I was born into a culture that taught, 'Your acts determine how God acts. So watch it!' My junior school headmaster used to enter class and call out, 'Hands up. Who wants to earn his ticket to heaven today?' Of course, we all did. A forest of hands usually volunteered for whatever errand he had in mind.

This lower-case god had done so little for me that if I didn't do it all myself, and do it right, there would be hell to pay. Consequently, my so-called good actions were to inspire god actions. Preferably nice ones. I was no fool. By the time I left for secondary school, I knew how to twist this god's cruel arm right up his cold back. And in that humble way that most religious folk have, I also grew to be quite proud of my technique.

'See how good I am, world! And you, god – are you watching? How about an eternal pat on the back?'

When the curtain fell in between life's scenes, the private backstage moments were uneasy. A glance in a mirror to check if my 'public make-up' was intact usually revealed the biggest two-faced hypocrite to strut the world stage.

I well remember my sheer relief in the early hours of a cold January morning in 1972. I had just discovered the God of the Bible. He was nothing like the miserable, hell-dangling deity I grew up with. Here was this amazing God of love who had already acted to secure my salvation, through Christ on the cross. I just needed to accept it. All I had to do was to accept him and his gift, and put his plan for my life into action. It was as clear as black-on-white in his Book.

> For it is by grace that you have been saved, through faith – and this not from yourselves, it is a gift of God – not by works, so that no-one can boast. For we are God's workmanship, created in Christ Jesus to do good works . . . (Eph 2:8–10).

Salvation by works

I used to be so proud of my righteous acts. Then, my mother-in-law, who had an Isaiah way with words, said they were no better than 'filthy rags' (Is 64:6).

Occasionally, my righteousness slipped, especially when

my vivid imagination insisted on placing my shopkeeper mother-in-law in close proximity to her bacon slicer.

My conversion eventually solved my arrogance (not to mention my in-law problems). I realised that I could never do anything that was pure and good. Not as long as I feared for my eternal soul. Secretly, a good act was another spiritual brownie point. Everything was tainted and dirty. I imagined standing in heaven, proudly declaring that I had made it under my own steam.

Boasting! With utmost humility, of course.

When God converted my thinking, I saw one thing with crystal clarity: my self-righteous robe was less than Persil white. It was even worse than a 'filthy rag'.

I realised that my mother-in-law and Isaiah were being kind.

Amazingly, the saving came first. My good acts followed. They were not to twist God's arm. Now there was no need. From this point onwards, my good works could be simply and purely works of gratitude.

Joshua likewise saw God's action first. Joshua's Act Two then flowed in thanks.

Here was a God who began preparing his people's salvation, generations before, through Abraham, Isaac and Jacob. That was Act One, Scene One. Scene Two saved his starving people from famine by providing them with a haven in Egypt through Joseph and his multi-coloured coat story. Scene Three saved them through the Exodus sea after Scene Two turned sour. This was a God who acted first no matter what the actions of his people. And he could do no other for he was, and is, the God of love.

Act One of love produced Joshua's Act Two of gratitude.

No repeat performances

Joshua had a cast-iron resolve never again to play the puppet at the end of someone else's strings. No way was Joshua going back to bondage. Nor was anybody else in his charge.

This resolve is mirrored in modern Israel, though for different reasons. On the El Al flight back home, my black-suited orthodox Jewish neighbour treated me like a fillet of forbidden pork. To be honest, I wasn't too surprised. Israelis are among the warmest of people when they get to know you, but on first meeting . . . !

'Why?'

That's what I dared to ask another Jew later in the flight. This one had gone out of his way to befriend me, to make up for the freeze of his fellow compatriot. Before long, we had become bosom buddies through discovering common roots in Manchester. So, I risked the question.

'Why are you people so prickly at first meeting?'

'Remember where we've been, my friend,' he said with an expansive Jewish shrug. 'After the Warsaw Ghetto; after the Final Solution and Auschwitz and Treblinka; after we fought the world for our land, endured six-day wars and the terrorist bombs, we said, "Never again!" '

And Joshua was one of the first to say it.

Once he stood in victory beyond the Exodus sea, there was no way he would be willing to return to the failure of bondage.

One of our greatest motivations is the realisation of what God has freed us from. Also, the bondage that others are still enduring. Further impetus to cross our Jordans comes in knowing that God can only free them and the world through you and me. And Joshua saw the truth of that for himself and his people. We are called to join in wholeheartedly with Joshua's sentiments, and shout: 'Never again!'

Of course, those with a realistic view of human nature will challenge: 'What never?'

And Joshua's honesty would shine through: 'Well, hardly ever.'

Of course he was no archangel.

And here, perhaps, we find our closest rapport with the Joshua drama, and a bit of encouragement for lesser mortals.

Through it we see yet another lesson from our Mr Motivator.

Encores are fun but hold up performance

Joshua was only human. Of course, he gave old temptations and fears a few encores. This was certainly true as he wandered ever nearer to the Jordan River. Replaying seductions always stops us going forward. It did with Joshua. How many extra minutes, hours or even days he spent in the wilderness as a result is not revealed. What is certain is that God had to spend precious time giving his Old Testament saviour a long pep talk before he got action.

'Come on, Joshua, stop doubting me. Pull yourself together. Trust in my power. I need you. Don't go AWOL after all we've been through. Be strong. Be very courageous. I'll be with you. Yes, even as I was with Moses. Go for it, my son. Go on' (Josh 1).

'He's a good boy, our Joshua,' as Nun and Mum probably confided in the past over their neighbour's tent pegs, 'but, Ai-yi-yi, a towering hero always he was not!'

There was the time, for instance, when he got it badly wrong. In effect, he dethroned God and crowned his boss. He decided that the Lord couldn't work without Moses.

Almost understandable in view of what had happened in the past. Moses must have seemed to merge with God at times. For a start, 'the glory of the Lord settled' on them for well over a month on Mount Sinai (Ex 24:13–18).

And then there were the special tent episodes.

Every time the Israelites stopped their wanderings, Moses would take cloth and animal hides and set up what he called the Tent of the Meeting. He did it outside the main camp. Joshua, a sort of verger or deacon, looked after the tent, and also the people who came to meet with the Lord. But there were special times when only Moses came. He and God would be outside, face to face as friends, while Joshua remained within.

Can you imagine some of the conversations he must have overheard!

Face to face with God?

Joshua might have helped us with a biblical conundrum.

No man can see the face of God and live, Moses was told in Exodus 33:20. However, nine verses earlier, it states that 'the Lord would speak to Moses face to face'.

To add to the confusion, in Numbers 12 we have Moses' sister and brother criticising Moses, and God bringing all three to account: 'With him,' the Lord spoke from the pillar of cloud concerning Moses, 'I speak face to face. . . . '

In some way, God took a form that Moses could tolerate. When God denied him sight of his face, it seems that Moses was asking to see the pure, undiluted glory of God.

It is, therefore, perhaps excusable that Joshua decided his boss was God's only mouthpiece. Consequently, when two elders who had not been anointed by Moses started to prophesy, Joshua demanded, 'Moses, my lord, stop them!'

'Are you jealous for my sake?' replied Moses. 'I wish that all the Lord's people were prophets and that the Lord would put his Spirit on them' (Num 11:26–29).

Definitely a put-down. One of those Whoops! moments in life. A foot-in-mouth *faux pas*. It may not have put Joshua on a par with the Great Train Robbers, but it does show that he was not exactly Mr Perfect. He would have been the first to support one of God's later stained heroes, St Paul, who wrote, 'I do not understand what I do. For what I want to do I do not do, but what I hate I do' (Rom 7:15).

Joshua was just as frail and fragile as you and I and Paul. He is most certainly somebody with whom we can identify. Make him into anything more, as Joshua did with Moses, and we too will deserve a put-down.

All this provides another strong inspiration for action. We, like Joshua, know this forgiving, encouraging God who has done so much for us. It seems only fair that we should do things for him. The bigger, the better.

Not only the gift of forgiveness spurs us on. There's also gratitude for making us less liable to tempting bondage.

The show must go on despite the encores

God's gracious helping hand is especially precious when what we most deserve is the back of his hand.

The devil laughs at our reprise of past failures. We dally with a temptation. You can almost hear the smirk, especially if it's one of the old weaknesses that had us in bondage for years before the Spirit of God came to our rescue.

Incredible, how temptation makes fools of us. Just for fun, we go surfing in the Exodus sea. Surprise! Surprise! A giant wave whisks us back across towards slavery! So easy to end in deep water. Sometimes, so hard to get our feet back on the ground . . . to stand in control . . . in victory.

But what to do?

A hint at the solution can be seen in a photo above my computer screen as I type. It's the standard snapshot for every Dead Sea bather. There I am, feet up, reading my book and sitting back in the salt-dense water. I'm a few miles below where Joshua crossed the Jordan. Looks good. But you try getting out of that position!

The feet won't come down because of the buoyancy. The hands are totally useless because they're holding that precious book. You're a helpless cork bobbing in the briny. Solution? Well, it took a couple of minutes, but first you submit to the situation. Next, you resist the rising panic, then gently kick for shore. Your rear end, eventually and thankfully, scrapes the sea bed. You can then scramble upright.

Dead Sea

Rounding the south-west shore of the plump, 48-mile long finger of the Dead Sea, locals pointed out human-size pillars of salt.

'Lot's wife!' they exclaimed secretively, as if I was the only tourist to be let in on this classified information.

We were just a short distance from ancient Sodom from where Lot and his wife fled (Gen 19). Mrs Lot disobeyed God, paused and looked back. She was showered with a chemical cocktail of salt potash, magnesium, and calcium chlorides and bromides.

These are the chemicals which make up a quarter of the Dead Sea's density, providing its extra buoyancy. A.R. Millard (*The New Bible Dictionary*) suggests that these chemicals ignited during an earthquake and 'caused the rain of brimstone and fire destroying Sodom and Gomorrah'.

Out of your depth in temptation? There's a similar soul-saving recipe.

'Submit yourselves, then, to God,' wrote New Testament

writer James. 'Resist the devil, and he will flee from you' (Jas 4:7).

That's exactly what Joshua did. And more besides.

He and Moses put distance between themselves and that which had held them in bondage. Of course, it left them in a wilderness for a time. But much closer to God. There are friendships and associations that imprison us by their low standards. Our only hope is to flee, even though it may leave us alone – except for God.

Temptations, of course, come not only from the past and outside but also from within. Joshua realised this earlier in life when he was nearly stoned to death by his own people on returning from his spying mission. He and Caleb had urged an invasion. The other ten spies disagreed. So did the rest (Num 14).

'Joshua, be reasonable,' the tempting would have started from those who swore they had his best interests at heart. 'Take a break. Put your feet up. You've had a hard forty days doing our dirty work. Time for a holiday, and we've got ages to deal with those giant problems in the Promised Land.' The sliding scale of seduction would have steepened until only the threat of violence was left.

When we cannot distance ourselves from temptations, our only refuge is within. It is the inner sanctuary for a heart-to-heart with the Lord. It is that place in which we refresh ourselves through his word. Where we put on the whole armour of God (Eph 6:10–18). It's that place we know his voice, his vision, his encouragement and his strength.

But within is also a source of temptation – our other selves.

This is especially true when we are at our strongest. We'll be meeting this and dealing with it later as Joshua fights for the promised city of Ai (Chapter 14).

No victory is gained without a fight. And Joshua was

certainly a fighter. So the question becomes: Any more for the fray?

This drama unfolding at the centre of civilisation is a script for Everyman's encouragement.

First, God's action is designed to impel Joshua and ourselves to greater things. Second, we should be spurred on by the memory of what the Lord has rescued us from. Third, with God's power we can overcome our frailties, just as Joshua did. We too can be heroes, with God's bravery. Fourth, God helps us override those reruns of failure so that we ride on towards victory.

And next, we will see an even more excellent inspiration . . . .

8
The Calling

'I am called!'

Joshua could shout it from mountain tops. Perhaps he did. Maybe the first hints came on Mount Sinai when Israel got her vocation. Wherever and whenever it was, this call, more than anything else, propelled him to the Jordan.

God's calling is the rocket fuel of our inner space. With it, we can boldly go where God's men and women *have* gone before. Without it, we rarely progress beyond launch-pad spectator, and our thrill can only be in the ventures of others. Yet, once we respond to God's whispered summons, not even the sky's the limit. These are the adventures of the enterprising star Joshua, and it could just as easily be you.

And it simply begins with a call.

'Take Joshua son of Nun, a man in whom is the spirit,' the Lord said to Moses, 'and lay your hand on him. Make him stand before Eleazar the priest and the entire assembly and commission him in their presence' (Num 27:18–19).

Call to emigrate

The Lord said to Abraham, 'Leave your country, your people and your father's household and go to the land I will show you' (Gen 12:1).

□□□

Of course, Joshua could have refused. You and I know that. Each one of us has stood on one or other of God's launch-pads. We've had that quiet still voice prompting us to climb aboard.

'Go on, my child,' it whispers. 'Give me this . . . go that way . . . give up that habit . . . do this for me . . . test me in this and just see if I will not open the windows of heaven and pour out my blessing on you' (see Malachi 3:10).

Without God, nothing

'Human excellence means nothing, unless it works with the consent of God' (Euripedes, *The Suppliant Woman*).

□□□

Joshua had the identical whispered voice in the wilderness.

'Thanks, Lord, but no thanks,' he could have replied. 'I've got a few goats set aside for my old-age pension. I'd rather thought of downshifting to camel driver, if you don't mind. Time for the young 'uns to take over. Put me down for a bit of Saturday school teaching, Lord, but nothing else. Okay?'

Two things would have followed this response. The divine whisper would have died in the inner silence, and God would have quietly and sadly moved on to choose somebody else. Second, Joshua's blessings would have dried up. Our man would have stepped out of God's will and into his own, and this is perhaps the greatest frustration our Lord endures.

He spends years apprenticing millions and ends up with a handful of qualified faithfuls. Many carry on in their own strength, only gradually realising that they failed to graduate. Had Joshua drowned the whisper and gone his own way, he would not have heard the tears of heaven and the wail of angels. He would have been too busy wandering in his own wilderness. He would have been living out his own selfish drama as one of life's two-faced performers. Acting. And he would have known it.

Call of Moses

'So now, go. I am sending you to Pharaoh to bring my people the Israelites out of Egypt' (Ex 3:10).

Ever listened to a public speaker who's scared, and his voice tremors with it? I was elected a town councillor in my pagan twenties. Every time I rose in the council chamber my voice would develop a nervous tremolo. It sounded as though I was on the point of bursting into tears at any moment.

The reason? I am not one of life's performers. I play the trumpet, passably on my own and atrociously before others. I juggle. In the study, with only the Utax photocopier for an audience, I'm brilliant. Five balls at one time. Seven on a good day (jugglers are like anglers when talking of catches). When it comes to the rare public performances, I go for the sympathy vote.

However, you ask me to preach. You invite me to give a day-long seminar on my topic. No problem. The voice is rock solid, firm, confident, assured. Billy Graham, watch out! Luis Palau move over. I have even been known to juggle in a family service.

Why?

Because I believe with all my heart that God has called me to do it – even the family service juggling. It's not a performance. It's a real-life vocation. And, what's more, I know it!

With such knowledge, you can rise above the might of Egypt's chariots. Amalekites can be slain. You can survive in a wilderness for forty years, cross a half-mile-wide river and direct a wayward world back to God. You can run a youth club, become a deacon, tell your friend how Jesus Christ came into your life, invite him or her to that church mission, feed the hungry, visit the sick, start that counselling course, even open a drug rehabilitation drop-in centre.

You want a life? Get a calling!

Advice to a son

'There is hardly anybody good for everything, and there's scarcely anybody who is absolutely good for nothing' (Lord Chesterfield, *Letters to His Son*, 2nd January, 1748).

Look into the eyes of your church youth, if you have any. Some sparkle with vision, but many more with boredom. In contrast, few young eyes in modern Israel are dull. They follow their leader, who normally packs a Kalashnikov automatic. Ever-ready for war. They're bright and alert. For they feel called. Ancient Israel under Joshua must have been the same.

But how do we discover a calling?

How can we be certain what God wants of us? Joshua gives us the answer.

A God's-eye view

First, Joshua identified the overall vision and grasped what God's salvation work was all about. This came, no doubt, as he helped Moses compile the first books of the Bible. They are shot through with God's cosmic salvation vision.

Stop an Israeli today and he will give you, in concise terms, exactly what he and his nation are doing. Drive into the West Bank and the Palestinian will be equally sure. Both have a calling. The rest of the world might quail on the sidelines, but not them. As I write, two young men from Hebron have just walked into Jerusalem's fruit market and blown themselves up killing and injuring dozens. Such is the strength of a calling.

A prophet's call

'Then I heard the voice of the Lord saying, "Whom shall I send? And who will go for us?" And I said, "Here am I. Send me!"' (Is 6:8).

Check the vision

Joshua, secondly, ensured that his calling was of God. He went to an authoritative guide – the Book of the Law, the first books of the Old Testament. And then he meditated on them day and night.

The two suicide bombers identified their calling apparently through village myth and a tradition primed by patriotism. They were assured that martyrdom, and the killing of infidel men, women and children, would take them straight to paradise. Once there, they could enjoy the forbidden earthly pleasures of wine and seventy-two virgins.

Joshua went to the word of God to discover what life and

death – and his life – were all about. Through it, God spoke to him about his calling.

Fair warning

'Vocations which we wanted to pursue, but didn't, bleed, like colours, on the whole scene of our existence' (Balzac).

□□□

The Jews have named the first five books the Torah. It's the Hebrew word for 'law' but it means far more. John Drane, in his excellent *Introducing the Old Testament*, writes of Torah, 'It really meant "guidance" or "instruction", and in the Old Testament the Law was the place to discover what men and women should believe about God, and what duties he required of them in return.'[1]

God's body

Joshua next saw the desire of God to have physical hands and feet on planet earth. He saw himself as a member of the body of people through whom God would work. He understood that he could frustrate God and his work by his absence.

Paul's call

'Now get up and stand on your feet. I have appeared to you to appoint you as a servant and as a witness of what you have seen of me and what I will show you' (Acts 26:16).

□□□

Is it not one of the greatest phenomena of creation that God chooses to rely on you and me? The Number One Person of the Universe relies on the six billionth and one or other of us. And not for a moment is it ever as impersonal as that sounds. He knows and loves not only each one of his created billions, but every hair of our individual heads (Mt 10:30).

I worry about God sometimes. I wonder how he copes. I know he's almighty. Yes, he's all powerful and all knowing. But still I worry. He must be very sad when he comes to work that part of the body which involves me. He sends out a signal and that limb of his body limps, or even ignores the call.

I had a friend once who suffered from locked-in syndrome. She was as bright as a button inside. If you could stay around long enough, a halting sentence would eventually escape word by word from her. Every now and then, she could get her body to obey a directive. She and God got on well. They swapped experiences in prayer. He told her he had the same problem with his body, from time to time.

Anybody there?

The fourth way Joshua discovered his calling was in a close relationship with God. He asked for specific guidance.

Now, God's general guidance comes, of course, from his guidebook. It's fine for pointing out the overall direction of what God wants to do in our lives. It also defines what he doesn't want us to do. For instance, as a vicar I know that it's wrong to have an affair with my Sunday school superintendent. However, it's okay for me to sleep with the church organist – but only because she doubles as the vicar's wife.

The Bible is great for generalities about what, and what not, to do. It's poor on the specific what-do-I-do-now? type of direction. Which job? Whom should I marry? Is God telling me to be a church visitor? Should I speak in tongues, or interpret, or heal?

Joshua was more fortunate in this respect than us. The

Book told him specifically that he was to lead God's people into the Promised Land. However, just like you and I, he still had to fathom the when and how and where of it.

Ask no more

'Blessed is he who has found his work; let him ask no more blessedness' (Thomas Carlyle, *Past and Present*, 1843).

Joshua did this by getting advice. He sent in spies. No doubt he listened to his co-leaders. The more heads and ears in touch with God the better our chances of hearing what he has to say. Joshua then took the circumstances into consideration. God led him to employ the open/closed door principle; to test various avenues of advance. Of course, in his case it was not doors, but a river.

Finally – and only finally – he would have listened to that inner feeling of what he thought the Lord was saying. He knew from past experience of getting things wrong that the last thing he should pay attention to was his own heart and instincts. They were too fallible.

Then, he let God's people lay hands on him.

Body ministry

Joshua immersed himself in God's main channel of guidance: the body of the church. God's people.

It is very rarely, if ever, just you and God. He might know and love every hair of your head, but God still does things involving a lot of hairy heads. God loves togetherness. More hands make light work. More accurately, more hands bring to light the work of God. That's why Joshua and God were content when the church representative, the priest Eleazar, laid hands on him.

Chosen to be instruments

'You did not choose me, but I chose you and appointed you to go and bear fruit' (Jn 15:16).

'But God chose the foolish things of the world to shame the wise; God chose the weak things of the world to shame the strong' (1 Cor 1:27).

What we need today is a lot more hands laying on a lot more people. God's people are needed to identify callings and to help church individuals know where they should be. And that, if I may dare state it in these modern liberated individualistic days, should be with, or without, the individual's agreement.

As far as we can tell, Joshua was not invited to consider whether or not he would like to be called to take over from Moses. God directed the church to do it through Moses. Then the church did it. Joshua had the right to say 'no', but the church had the right to say 'go'.

'Just wait till we lay our hands on you!' It's a good directive to hasty individuals who think they are being called. Check it out with your church.

Joshua is now called to cross the Jordan.

Note

[1] John Drane, *Introducing the Old Testament* (Lion Publishing), p 29.

9
Take It or Leave It

'When are they going to cross this flippin' river?'

If this is your reaction, you have a reminder of how God must have felt at the time.

Remember, he had wanted them to cross the Jordan forty years before. This time he was nurturing and nudging his beloved people across.

It's another pointer to understanding the awful sadness of being God. Those in leadership, like Joshua, glimpse it briefly. It's yet another spur to keep the Lord's work on track. When we are obedient and keep to the Lord's timetable, it must lighten the blues of heaven. In fact, when God's people stepped into the river there must have been a rainbow of celebration and joy streaming over paradise.

* * *

'Wagons roll!'

'Westward ho!'

The orders were out. The camp roused. Joshua stood by the raging river as three million on carts, camels, asses and Shanks's pony shuffled in the dusty approaches to the

Jordan. None was too eager. For one thing, they feared getting too near God's holy ark, held aloft by the priests already by the water's edge (Josh 3:4).

And there was another caution: not all were deliriously happy about this river outing. Especially without a boat. They'd never seen water do strange things. A tiny minority, as children, had actually witnessed water spring from the desert's solid rock when Moses and that divine staff did their miraculous job (Ex 17:1–7). Still fewer had marched through the walled-up waters of the Exodus sea (Ex 14:22). They were now the few surviving forty- or fiftysomethings who had been under the fighting age of twenty when their elders had revolted and refused God's orders to take the Promised Land.

As for the rest, there were fervent mutterings.

Some prayed in faith. Most prayed for faith. Others just wondered in silence. In another age, they would be the ones who thought they might need their heads examining. Had they but known what was about to happen, there would have been a stampede of curiosity.

> . . . as soon as the priests who carried the ark reached the Jordan and their feet touched the water's edge, the water from upstream stopped flowing. It piled up in a heap a great distance away, at a town called Adam . . . (Josh 3:15–16).

Now, Joshua and God might have made things easier for us at this stage. As we noted in Chapter 3, miracles are hard to swallow in this day and age. Rational minds find them indigestible. Many thinkers in fact remove them from the menu whenever possible.

Joshua could have explained a little more clearly what actually happened. First, if this was a myth, he – or whoever wrote it later – could have hinted as such. But no. It is blatantly written as factual 'this-really-happened' history. In that case, he might have described the 'heaping up' of the Jordan more precisely. It would have helped limited rational minds. He might even have pointed us to some geographical cause or phenomenon.

For instance, in the old days, the Jordan meandered along its rift valley so much that it did occasionally undercut the banks on bends. These would then eventually cave in to dam the river. Also, there are earthquakes to consider. Joshua could have gone into all this to help the modern mind understand.

River of descending

The crossing of the Jordan took place between the present-day Adam Bridge and the Allenby Bridge, a little north of Jericho.

There is evidence of landslides and blockages in this area. The record books tell us that on 7–8th December 1267 the Jordan was dammed for sixteen hours by collapsed earth. This also happened in 1906 and 1927.

The Jordan was more likely to be blocked during the full flood of harvest season, for then the swifter torrent would do the most damage.

The river's name means 'descending'. It used to roar into the rift valley, plunging from its origins, 1,230ft above sea level at Lake Huleh, down to the lowest point on earth. This was the Dead Sea at 1,300ft below sea level. You can imagine the force it had as it roared past Adam and Jericho.

Today, of course, hi-tech water control schemes have tamed it into little more than a pleasant stream.

True, it would still have been a miracle. God would still have had to organise the blockage with divine accuracy.

But at least modern minds would not have been stretched to incredulity.

But no! Joshua was obviously in no mood to mollycoddle the moderns and intellectuals of his age, our age or any other age. He refused to tone down the supernatural. So too did God. He said to his servant, 'Today I will begin to exalt you in the eyes of all Israel, so that they may know that I am with you as I was with Moses . . .' (Josh 3:7).

In other words, this incredibly gracious God was going to duplicate his famous water miracle for this new generation. This God of the second chance would give a sign of his presence and power just as he had to the old generation who had passed through the divided Exodus sea.

'This is how you will know that the living God is among you . . .' (Josh 3:10).

Joshua is a take-it-or-leave-it man. So too is God. In blunt words, this is what the Lord might have said if we pressed him for an explanation: 'I want no mistake. This is a miracle to prove that I am with my people. This is to prove that what is now about to happen is not natural. It is beyond that. I don't want any talk of coincidences. I don't want people later saying, "Surprise! Surprise! Fancy the banks collapsing just at the right moment." No. I want you to see me. I want our enemies also to hear about this and quake in their sandals.'

Heathen fear

Putting the fear of God into people is considered a bit OTT – Old Testament Terrorism. Surely, the argument goes, all we need today is love – à la New Testament

A balanced biblical view stresses that we need both.

As I composed this chapter, I was called to visit Dave, a bereaved husband. A few hours before, his wife had died of lung cancer at forty-nine. He just wants a nice, quiet funeral. God never really entered the conversation, and when I brought up the Lord there was a puzzled shrug.

'Is he relevant to this funeral?' the gesture seemed to ask.

There was no fear of facing God. If there was such a being, all well and good. If not, what does it matter anyway?

Bearing in mind what I was in the middle of writing, I felt an urge to ask if he didn't have the slightest worry where he was going when he died. Didn't it bother him that one day there would be a Judgement Day? Was he not concerned about accounting for his life (2 Cor 5:10)? Wouldn't he like to know that God's love could save him?

Of course, I resisted the urge. In his grief, he wouldn't have heard. If he had, he would have dismissed me as an insensitive oaf. There might be a right time to talk, I pray, but even then Dave will struggle, unless God convicts him of his sin, and his need for a loving Saviour.

Naturally, human beings cannot fear God. That's what Martin Luther wrote. Apostle Paul in his letter to the Romans stated that we are dead in our sinful state, and on our way to hell.

God loves us so much that he will do anything to keep us out of such an eternity. He will send prophets to tell us how to escape. He'll send preachers and pastors. He'll even come himself, in his Son, and die an agonising death for our sins so that we might live. He will even go OTT, and try to terrorise us into our right senses. God loves us so much that he will do anything he can to keep us from an eternity of terror.

True, we still need to preach his love and forgiveness, for only then will men and women escape their own fears. But it does no harm at all – and possibly some good – to put the right fear of God into people's minds.

'. . . let us purify ourselves from everything that makes body or soul unclean, and let us be completely holy by living in awe [reverent fear] of God' (2 Cor 7:1, GNB).

Just to make sure nobody can wriggle out of the miraculous meaning, Joshua adds the final proof. He even repeats it to make sure it strikes home: 'The priests who carried the ark . . . stood firm on *dry ground* . . . the whole nation had completed the crossing on *dry ground*' (Josh 3:17).

Just for a paragraph, let's examine the river-blockage theory.

The waters stopped flowing immediately the priests dipped in a toe. We've all flip-flopped across a beach immediately after a wave recedes. Two hundred of us once walked across Morecambe Bay in Lancashire after the tide ebbed. Words like squishy, sinking sand, boggy, mushy are all fair descriptions. The Jordan, of course, would have been far worse. This was not so much sand as a valley-full of rich fertile soil, especially in the flooded areas. This was no seaside stroll. This would have rapidly turned into a monumental quagmire. It would have been several hundred yards across, and churned calf-deep by countless marching feet, hundreds of carts, and thousands of livestock. It would have been impassable within minutes.

It would have needed a second miracle to part the bog!

'Like it or lump it,' Joshua might write today, 'this is no myth. This is miracle. There is no natural explanation. It's the Exodus sea all over again. I'm giving you one more chance to accept that God loves you. He loves you even enough to suspend his normally rigorous natural laws so that you might be encouraged and strengthened. He wants you to know he's with you.'

We do our world no favours today when we explain away

the supernatural. We merely bury God and faith in the quagmire that is left.

I am so grateful that these days I belong to a Joshua church. There are indications that this is happening in other denominations besides mine. It has, of course, not always been so. For most of my ministry, Joshua-types were humoured as quaint and old-fashioned. They were kept hidden on the margins of national church life. Centre-stage, the myth-merchants sold God and the faith short by trying to remodel them for the tastes of modern secular minds. But today, a new Spirit is blowing. Now, we are increasingly led by men and women who let God's word shape their minds. Those minds who tried to reshape God's word – and some did it from the best of motives – are now either in retirement or retreating to the margins of church life.

A church which faithfully presents this Joshua God may yet strike awe into modern hearts. The world desperately needs to know the right fear of God, just as much as those in Canaan days.

Whatever happened that day at the Jordan, it certainly terrified all the Amorite and Canaanite kings. And remember, kings reigned by personal might in those days. We're talking strong men here. Men who could not afford to show fear lest they lose their crowns. Men who certainly wouldn't tremble at mere coincidental caving in of river banks.

' . . . their hearts melted and they no longer had the courage to face the Israelites' (Josh 5:1).

Lest we forget

We human beings have poor memories. There are too many doubts for faith always to be triumphant. Yet we do try hard. We have God's word. We have the Holy Communion remembrance service. We surround ourselves with symbols lest we forget. Yet we do.

Stones of remembrance

Three flat stones stood one on top of the other against the red mountains of the Jordan-Israel border on the way down to Eilat. Scratched on the bottom one was '17 killed by terrorist bomb'.

Further along, another small tower of stones marked the spot where four joyriders died as their car somersaulted from the narrow tarmac strip into the desert.

In 2,800 kilometres of driving around Israel I must have seen a pillar of stones at least every 10 kilometres.

In Britain, we tend to lay bouquets at death scenes. When Diana, Princess of Wales, died, the nation was all but engulfed in flowers. We place a memorial or anniversary sentence in the evening paper's personal column. In Israel, the Jews pile up stones in remembrance. Go to any cemetery, and you'll find a pebble or two on the gravestone. It is a simple statement: 'I've called. I've remembered.'

One of the last shots in the award-winning film *Schindler's List* is a moving illustration. Hundreds of Jewish survivors of the Holocaust and their relatives file past their wartime saviour's memorial. They quietly and tearfully place small pebbles on it.

God began the practice – lest we forget him and his saving acts.

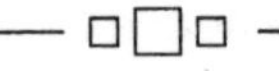

God and Joshua knew the same was true for the Old Testament church. So they set about reinforcing the Jordan miracle in the time-honoured way. A wayside memorial was erected. Joshua commanded that a man be chosen from each of the twelve tribes to carry a stone from the Jordan bed where the ark had stood. The stones were to be set up in the west bank camp at Gilgal. When future generations came to ask about them, they would be told, 'Israel crossed the Jordan on dry ground. For the Lord your God dried up the Jordan before you until you had crossed over' (Josh 4:20–24).

Joshua arranged for another twelve stones to be placed where the priests stood with their ark. Here's another reason why this story is no myth. Almost as though he guessed some might try to rationalise away this act of God, he added, 'And they are there to this day' (Josh 4:9).

Check it out

The Book of Joshua invites readers to check it out. 'Go and see the stones of remembrance yourself. They are there to this day.'

The apostle Paul did the same. After a different miracle and in another age, but still addressing the same sceptical human trait, he writes of the resurrection appearances of Jesus Christ, '. . . he appeared to more than five hundred of the brothers at the same time, most of whom are still living . . .' (1 Cor 15:6).

Like Joshua, Paul is saying, 'If you don't believe what we are saying, you can check for yourselves. Just to prove that this is no myth or old wives' tale, go and see the memorials; go and quiz the witnesses to the events. They are still there as we write.'

Love for all, no matter whom

Here begin the confessions of a Christian book writer. Joshua teaches me a valuable lesson at this point. Sinner though I am, there are certain types of sinners for whom I have a natural antagonism.

The honest-to-no-god atheist I can cope with. No problem. I love witches, occultists and even Satanists. I have ministered to some for a number of years. Give me the down-and-outs of society any time. I'll feed and clothe them. I'll spend hours with them. But sit me next to a doubting priest or bishop and, somehow, I lose it. Charity flies out of the window and my theological teeth fly for the throat.

But Joshua was different. And no doubt God is, too.

Joshua seems so gentle and loving when he addresses potential sceptics with, '. . . and they are there to this day.' And yet he is just as loving when it comes to the dregs of society . . . as we are about to see in the next chapter. He probably had sinners of all kinds flocking to him. For he mirrored the patience and love of the One who was to be his New Testament namesake.

My prayer is that I'll eventually get there. You can join me in an Amen, if it applies to you.

10

How to Manage – Part 1

The following conversation, or something like it, must have happened on the other side of the Jordan. Human nature almost guarantees it.

Among the troops preparing to attack the first Canaanite stronghold of Jericho, two soldiers meet. SETH is smiling (though not for long). DAN wears a painful expression as he mumbles the grave news to his fellow-in-arms. The response is explosive.

SETH: Joshua wants to do what!?
DAN: Circumcise you.
SETH [*wincing*]: He can't be serious! You have to be joking!
DAN: Every man under forty . . . [*tears spring to his eyes*] with a flint knife!
SETH: No chance! He'll have to go.
DAN: Sorry, my old mate. It's the other way round.
SETH: How do you mean?
DAN: You have the chop, or you're in for the chop, and you're out.
SETH: But why, for heaven's sake?
DAN: Precisely!
SETH: Eh?
DAN: It's for heaven's sake. The Lord's given Joshua his orders.

SETH: Couldn't Joshua ask for a second opinion?
DAN: Apparently, it's for our sakes, too.
SETH [*looking hopeful*]: Tell him he doesn't have to do it for my sake. I really won't mind.
DAN: It's something to do with good management – sharing the vision.
SETH [*with urgent emphasis*]: I share it! Whatever it is! [*now shouting.*] I SHARE IT! Honestly! I don't need it engraving on me with a flint knife!
DAN [*quietly*]: It appears you do.

Are you still sitting comfortably? It's not such a relaxing tale, is it? But it certainly grabs the attention. That's why God and Joshua chose the topic.

They now give us a superb lesson on how to manage the most difficult of situations in life. Whatever our circumstances – at work, at play, in church – this is for us. This is for those times when we feel so utterly out of our depth. You can even extract some principles to use around the home.

'I don't know how I'm going to manage!' is our cry at times. It was probably the Hebrew cry as well.

'Well, before we go to war,' Joshua and the Lord seem to say, 'we'll take a break and throw around a few ideas.'

That's precisely what they did in between the crossing of the Jordan and attacking Jericho with their brass band instruments. They took a crash course in how they were going to manage.

Get the vision, share the vision

The first rule of life management they were taught was simple: get the vision of where you're going. Rule number two: share the vision with others. And these two rules are not made for breaking. They work in whatever sphere they are applied – even in the home. If there are no targets to aim at, you won't hit anything.

The Lord, with Joshua's help, envisions Israel: 'Take centre-stage as my stars. Shine out to save a lost world.' Such was their mission statement, but how to impress it upon them? How to share it?

This is where circumcision came in.

This would leave them in no doubt. It was originally God's seal of approval on Abraham and his offspring (Gen 17). It simply stated, 'Those so marked belong to me.'

It reminded the people that their reproductive organs were not the 'be-all and end-all' of living. Their source of all life was beyond. Consequently, the human stem of life should be so marked that they never forgot that truth. It further reminded them that God would keep his people safe and well. He kept his end of the bargain through Isaac and Jacob, his twelve sons, and even in Egypt when it all went wrong. He sent Moses on a rescue mission.

The covenant held firm until Israel reneged on it. She declared her independence. She disobeyed divine orders to enter the Promised Land, and the agreement lapsed. So too did the physical sign of the contract. In short, God was saying, 'Stop marking yourselves as mine. You want to be your own bosses, that's your choice. Just don't expect my seal of approval.'

But all that was a rebellious generation before. Now, it was a new age and a new people and a new land. Their covenant with their ever-patient God was to be revived. So too was the sign.

'Make flint knives,' the Lord told Joshua, 'and circumcise the Israelites again . . . .' When this was completed, they remained in the camp until they were healed. Then the Lord said to Joshua, 'Today I have rolled away the reproach . . .' (Josh 5:9). To mark the special occasion they called their campsite 'Rolled Away' – Gilgal.

First, get the vision. Second, share it, even though this can be painful. Many will not want you to cut into their settled comfort. There will be protests for almost as many reasons as there are individuals. However, we humans, deep down, do love a cause, and for a good one we will rise up. Israel certainly did.

Vision and revision

But what next? Effective management demands repetition. Regular revision is needed.

For Israel, this was to be the Passover (Josh 5:10). This was the reminder of the last plague in Egypt when God's wrath passed safely over Hebrew homes while visiting death on the eldest child in Egyptian homes. This would annually jog the national memory.

'I saved you,' God tells them through it. 'You are my people. You are saved for a purpose.' Not a bad motto for his New Testament people either.

And there is more. God provided a daily reminder: a land overflowing with milk and honey, the fruit of their covenant.

'The day after the Passover . . . they ate some of the produce of the land . . . the manna stopped the day after' (Josh 5:11–12).

The land itself was to be an ever-present reminder of the God who provides for his special people.

Why milk and honey?

Imagine: you've decided to emigrate and are on the look-out for a new land. You get Canaan's stone brochure to browse.

Would you honestly have been attracted by fountains of milk and avalanches of honey? A land overflowing with the stuff. Would you have been sold?

Modern estate agents wouldn't use that language to sell a small property in Britain, never mind a whole country.

To the Israelites, however, it sounded like heaven.

Consider where they had been for forty years. The way

the winds have carved the Negev is breathtaking, and the stark dusty barrenness of the Wilderness of Zin is beautiful. All this is providing you're driving an air-conditioned hire car and not a flock of goats in the 100° degree heat. Then, all you yearn for is a decent pasture, even just a few yellowing grass blades. Anything to keep alive your milk and food source.

Milk was the staple diet of the Israelites. A special delicacy was curdled milk. The best treat of all was cream mixed with a scrape of precious honey. That was nectar.

Then, along comes God and tells you that he has a land overflowing with both milk and honey. Irresistible!

It has been well said that 'managers make things happen, through people'.

God never does anything else. He did it through his Old Testament nation, through his New Testament disciples and church, and he certainly isn't going to change now. As he continues to manage the world's salvation, he chooses to do it only through you and me. A sobering thought.

Getting the vision and sharing the vision is only the start. Modern management-speak loves acronyms. Here's an appropriate Old Testament one:

Joint teamwork
Overview of the team
Share
Handle appropriately
Utmost for his highest
Appreciation.

Joint teamwork

Joshua knew that there were no one-man bands in God's orchestra. Even a great leader like himself was not expected to take on the world single-handedly, which is why he had three million assistants. The lesson of teamwork came early while still an assistant manager.

Moses was on the point of burnout after the Exodus. Then, father-in-law Jethro came to visit. As we noted in the 'Hebrew civil service' panel in Chapter 7, he was appalled to find Moses acting as judge, jury and general ombudsman for the masses.

'Why do you alone sit as judge, while all these people stand round you from morning till evening?' he asked his son-in-law. 'What you are doing is not good . . . you will only wear yourselves out . . . select capable men from all the people – men who fear God, trustworthy men who hate dishonest gain – and appoint them as officials over thousands, hundreds, fifties and tens' (Ex 18:14–21).

Joshua had desert-tested this theory for forty years, and he was still using it as he prepared to take the Promised Land. 'So Joshua ordered the officers of the people: "Go through the camp and tell the people . . ."' (Josh 1:10).

Managers make things happen through people. Cutting through the jargon, management is about making the most of who and what you've got, to get the maximum result, with the minimum of effort.

I once knew a vicar who ran around dog-tired like a headless chicken, burning the candle at both ends while crying over spilt milk on his last legs. He was shattered, held together by a thread, bone-tired, knocked-up, knocked down, knocked out and knocked sideways. He was more weary and mixed up than the metaphors in the last two sentences, and it happened because I – I mean *he* – thought he had to do everything. He learned the hard way that God makes things happen through teams of people.

Legs should not try running apart from the body of Christ. On their own they always flop.

From a school noticeboard . . .

'None of us is smarter than all of us.'

□□□

Overview of the team

Having a God's-eye view is essential. But once you have the overall vision, and have ensured that the team knows it, you then need an overview of how your team will work.

Groups, especially churchy ones, have a bad name. Comic wags trot out the old favourite about 'a camel is a horse designed by a committee'.

'If you want something done properly,' they huff, 'do it yourself!'

Committees are often judged too harshly because they rarely get the chance to grow up. They seldom get beyond the Adrian Mole stage of acne and puberty. Joshua saw the various stages of group working from Egypt onwards. He knew that groups have to mature in their own time.

First, there is the childlike stage of enthusiasm mixed with fear.

At this early point for Israel, Moses, aided by Joshua, provided good parenting and direct leadership. They autocratically set out the purpose: 'we're leaving Egypt'. They gave secure directions: 'through the Exodus sea'. All groups, no matter what size, at first need the security of firm leadership to overcome initial anxieties.

A bit of good firm mothering ensures that the group makes it to rebellious adolescence.

Israel did eventually reach this stage. You could tell simply by tuning in to their griping: 'We didn't realise it would be so hard. If you don't play it my way, I'm taking my ball home!'

Or in more scriptural language, 'Why did you bring us up out of Egypt to make us and our children and livestock die of thirst?' (Ex 17:3).

The Israelites were getting fed up with those who were making the rules. They wanted to go back home. Good leaders should expect disenchantment after the first flush of enthusiasm. Moses and Joshua were still learning.

'They're almost ready to stone me,' protested Moses.

If the adolescent teenager gives the human race a bad name, that goes doubly for immature church committees. Both are bodies of conflicting contradictions. Both strive for independence yet do not have the experience and maturity to be so. They can't get their own way, so they become bored and sulk.

And yet, this phase of life can often be one of the best. This is a highly creative time. New ideas can pop out like teenage acne. Here, we learn to cope with each other. We see how to channel conflict and anger to our best advantage. Just as no adult can bypass this stage, nor can our team. And we also need to remember that committees may often regress back to lip-pouting, especially if the team's task changes, or new members join.

How do you manage a lumbering, awkward, rebellious adolescent? *Hasty answer*: You pick up a chair for protection and a big whip. *Considered answer*: With a great deal of sensitivity and care. The chairman of such a church committee will not be the blunt, unthinking autocrat. Though that approach helped in the insecure starting stage, now it can damage the development of the group and the people in it.

Moses eventually got the right idea. He listened to the grumbles and the dissatisfactions over lack of water and thirst in his group, and he took counsel: ' . . . take in your hand the staff with which you struck the Nile . . . . Strike the rock, and water will come out of it for the people to drink' (Ex 17:5–6).

Modern management, of course, has a little problem about taking counsel from God. Worldly managers therefore advise group members to talk to each other, while the leadership eavesdrops. Every member needs to speak and listen, no matter what is said. All views, no matter how rebellious, should be aired. Otherwise, the future will never be owned by the group. No teenager is going to live his father's life. No group will click its heels and play 'follow my leader' for life.

Church group members also need to listen to each other, but without forgetting their distinct advantage over secular committees – the divine connection.

A time comes when puberty passes, the acne begins to heal, and adulthood is reached. This can take a little time, and patience is required. For Joshua and Israel it took forty years, and even then it needed major miracles. Church committees do not generally take this long. Not always.

It has to be noted that teams need to be manageable. Three million is rather on the large side, even when broken into small groups. Consider, for example, what happens when, say, Fred and Sam get together. That's one group.

Then Jack joins them. You still have one group of three people. But you also now have three subgroups – Fred and Sam, Fred and Jack and Sam and Jack. This group has four relationships.

Get another five joining the group and you have 247 possible inter-relationships in the group. I used to belong to a church council meeting with forty-three members, and each decision we made was hailed as a modern miracle.

Generally, the smaller the number, the easier and more numerous the resolutions. However, your team has to be big enough to represent most opinions.

Joshua was always careful to ensure that he followed the Lord's command to draw representatives from all tribes. He also ensured that his leadership was appropriate. Jumping ahead a little to the conquering and division of Canaan between the tribes, it says, 'Then Joshua sent the people away, each to his own inheritance' (Josh 24:28).

Unlike Joshua, most will find this the hardest type of leadership to exercise. It means giving up your power to others. Joshua got to the point of handing over control to those under him. He worked himself out of a job, which is the aim of all group leaders. The trouble, of course, is that leaders don't like redundancy. They hang on, thinking themselves to be a steadying anchor. The group, meanwhile, thinks he's a lead weight.

Why?

Quips about committees

'Committees . . . keep minutes and lose hours' (Milton Berle).

'They are the . . . unwilling, picked from the unfit, to do the unnecessary' (Richard Harkness).

'We always carry out by committee anything in which any one of us alone would be too reasonable to persist' (F. C. Colby).

We recognise that every one of the above has more than a grain of truth. Yet, if the simple rules in our chapter are followed, committees can work. Just knock a few heads together in the right way. Far better than the lonely process of knocking your own head against a brick wall.

A team that has reached this third stage will have hammered out the solutions to its problems. The members will have done it. Not the leader. It is group power that has achieved, and the good leader will only have been there to aid this process. He will be like the parent hovering in the background of his adult offspring's independent life. The power of his group, not his power, will have succeeded, and the various members will know this. As a consequence, they will own the group's decisions and actions.

When a group reaches this stage in industry, its leader may only drop in occasionally. Merely for an update. He might perhaps briefly arbitrate in a nagging snag. Otherwise, other members of the group take the lead, depending on which expertise or direction is needed. Only if the group gets a new task or has a radical membership shake-up will the leader take over the reins again, and then only to give direction until conflicts have been successfully resolved.

A settled third stage leads to the final bliss of maturity. This is when the group is working at its peak. Quite a few church committees do manage this, despite rumours to the contrary.

At this stage, the goal or vision is being fully realised. In the case of Israel and Joshua, this was to last for almost a generation. They did succeed in being God's people centre-stage of the world. 'Israel served the Lord throughout the lifetime of Joshua and of the elders who outlived him and who had experienced everything the Lord had done for Israel' (Josh 24:31).

In Israel's maturity, Joshua's leadership was almost non-existent. Approaching 110, he had done his bit. The gratifying thing to note is that, despite his absence, despite even his death, the group carried on to achieve the original vision.

That's true leadership. Biblical leadership.

Joshua is probably one of the few world-class leaders to have truly worked himself out of a job. *So successful was he that they never appointed a successor*. In that respect, he outshone even his boss. The idea was that Israel, set up in their various tribal lands, would allow the Lord to be their leader. Amazingly, it worked for a generation, before God's judges had to be sent in (Judg 2:16).

11

How to Manage – Part 2

Get the vision. Pass it on. Work jointly in teams and possess the overview of what makes them tick. Next in our J.O.S.H.U.A. acronym . . .

Share

Joshua had a remarkable rapport with his team. Obviously, it stemmed from shared experiences and adventures over a forty-year partnership. No sharing. No partnership. And it takes time. Hopefully, in our case, shorter than forty years (but who knows?).

Joshua's group certainly shared honestly even when it came to confrontation. As noted already, Gad, Reuben and half the tribe of Manasseh were able to tell Joshua that their families were not crossing (Josh 1:12–18). A shared trust and acceptance must have existed to reach a solution in such a critical conflict. And such resolution comes only from listening groups. Sharing groups communicate with each other, while sharing the same goals.

Joshua also felt he could share anything with his people and they would do it.

'Get ready to cross a raging river.' And they did.

'Lay your life on the line and go and spy out Jericho.' No problem.

'Priests, take up the ark and march into the torrent.' No sooner said than done.

'Stay in the middle while we get across.' They stayed put.

'Trumpeters, be ready to lead the charge on Jericho.' They began warming up.

And therein lies the other vital ingredient of sharing groups: it's never the faithful few. Each member has a job and shares the responsibility.

The only passenger over the Jordan was the ark.

Handle appropriately

Already, we have seen Joshua's flexibility with the two and a half tribes. They talked it through and eventually agreed that while the families remained, their fighting men would take the lead in battle (Josh 1:12–18).

Now, consider the coming battle. There must have been a massive about-turn as they came to their first Canaan battle – Jericho.

They've got 600,000 soldiers and their generals camped to the east of Jericho. They've had years to plan their strategy. Some can still remember beating the Amalekites. Others boast of putting Sihon and Og to flight. Swords have been sharpened, spears pointed, chariots greased and horses and camels brought to peak condition. The SAS-type strategists probably used their ramble through the Jordan basin to debrief the two Jericho spies, gleaning every titbit of geography and terrain of use. Battle siege plans are prepared and the army is resting, just waiting for the final word from Joshua. Then it comes . . .

'March around the city once with all the armed men,' he tells them.

'Well, erm, yes,' you can imagine the nervous response.

'Actually, Joshua, we'd thought of something else. But, well, o-kay. . . . '

'Do this for six days.'

'Six?'

'Have seven priests with rams' horns in front of the ark.'

'Yes. The ark's good. We'd thought of that. Rally the troops, and all that. But the priests . . . ?'

'On the seventh day, march around the city seven times, with the priests blowing the ram's horn trumpets – '

'Excuse me. Did you say trumpets? Could you repeat – '

'When you hear them sound a long blast on the trumpets, make all the people give a loud shout; then the wall of the city will collapse and the people will go up, every man straight in' (Josh 6:2–5).

The above conversation might have happened in a modern church committee. We can be certain it did not happen in Joshua's planning group. Subtract the imagined interjections from the strategists and you just have the Lord's orders.

Team power and God's power

Observant, questioning readers will have noticed by now that a contradiction has crept into our look at modern management.

In Chapter 10, we stressed teamwork. Now, in this chapter, Joshua lays down the law and the team seems redundant. No discussion. Just dictatorship.

The answer comes in the one major difference between a Christian team and a secular management team: God.

In the business world, the group is god, so long as it stays within the company's overall vision. The Christian group, however, recognises that there is a power beyond it. A directing, guiding power.

God does this through those he calls to be prophets

(Eph 4:11). The Joshuas of God's people have been gifted to pass on the thoughts of God's mind.

Such messages are not so much up for debate as testing. Here the group comes into action. We need to weigh carefully what is said (1 Cor 4:19).

Joshua had been tested long and hard. We need to do the same to those who would be present-day prophets. The test of Joshua was simple: did things happen as he claimed God had told him? Well, the waters parted!

Church teams should listen to each other. But, chiefly, they must listen to God through each other.

And lest this all sounds too heavenly minded, prophets are candidly in short supply in today's church. We need to research this area as a matter of priority.

Of course, in the meanwhile, we listen to each other, trying prayerfully to detect God's word and guidance in human sounds.

By this time, such was the trust and shared vision and fellowship in the group that Joshua simply had to say it, and it was accepted. Now that is handling matters appropriately, with flexibility and willingness to adapt. Even the best plans of military men oft go astray. So, too, do church plans, home plans, and even industrial blueprints.

The most effective group is the one whose members can best adapt to changing situations. No matter how odd. The group that succeeds is the one which expects things to change, and is never surprised by change.

Utmost for his highest

Of course, I've pinched this from the classic work, *My Utmost for His Highest*, by Oswald Chambers, my favourite book of inspiration. Joshua could have written it as well. He demanded nothing but the best from his team – and he got it.

But how do you get a team performing at peak efficiency; giving the very best quality? Answer: Let it work towards the highest goals it can manage. Then, give it all the resources it needs to achieve them. But do it the Hebrew way. Subdivide your goals into small manageable tasks, and try to give the team a victory early on.

'The world's our goal,' is a rough summary of what Moses told Joshua, 'but first, have a crack at the Amalekites. I'll provide you with all that you need.' Then he stood on a nearby hill and kept the Lord's staff aloft for victory (Ex 17:8–16).

One of the best ways to achieve early victory is to worry a problem into a solution. Worry your problems into solutions and you will have success. Early success encourages people to try their utmost. We all love to be on the winning side. Israel would never have taken on Canaan, not even the Jordan, had Joshua and God not given them signs of success. Joshua and God gave them these successes simply by working in the background. They ensured good lines of communication and a streamlined organisation which could make for speedy decisions and crack problems.

Appreciation

The spies Joshua sent ahead into Jericho returned and experienced job satisfaction overnight. Joshua and three million souls moved out to the Jordan simply on their word. The officers of the camp felt tremendously useful as they ran through the camp whispering, 'It's D-day at dawn.'

One decoding clerk at wartime Bletchley Park worked throughout 4th June 1944, ready for D-day the following day. At the last minute, it was postponed because of bad weather. She knew that D-day would then be scheduled for

6th June. As a result she stayed on at Bletchley during the following day.

'Nobody asked us to stay,' she said. 'It was sort of expected because we were in on the secret. They thought we might have been kidnapped or something. But, to be honest, I would have stayed for the rest of the week because we all knew that our work was vital. We appreciated that, and we also knew that the high-ups appreciated us. Churchill was always visiting and telling us how vital our work was.'

Who has the real vision?

Imagine two Israelites detailed by Joshua to pick up large stones from the dried-up River Jordan.

'What are you doing in this part of the world?' asks a passer-by.

'We're building a memorial to God's saving work,' says one.

'We *are* God's memorial!' exclaims the other.

Which one has the real vision?

□□□

Joshua was definitely a Churchillian encourager. He supported in the background while the priests held up the water. Later, the trumpeters and the people would share the glory of Jericho's falling walls.

When a team knows that the leader serves them for their benefit, it tries that much harder. The same happens when team members are encouraged to work for each other, and appreciate each other's contributions.

Do you want success? At church? At work? Even at home? Then J.O.S.H.U.A! **J**oint teamwork. Get the **O**verview of the goal and of how teams work. **S**hare totally. **H**andle situations and people appropriately. Give your **U**tmost for the Most High. **A**ppreciate each other.

The team of ex-Egyptian slaves resting at Gilgal near Jericho did all this. And they were to become worldbeaters. They were supremely confident. They had seen what had happened in the past and what the Lord had done for them. They were proud to belong to this special people. They were a dynamic whole, working with a joint sense of purpose and with the confidence of winners. No wonder the enemy were shaking in their cities. ' . . . a great fear of you has fallen on us,' a prostitute called Rahab told the spies (Josh 2:9).

When we modern people of God trust at the same level as the old people of God, we too will repeat their success. When we supplement the power of God with his biblical patterns of management, as did Israel, the world opposed to God will tremble.

Rebels retuned

Groups in loops go nowhere. Teams with wrong dreams blur the vision. Squads at odds flop. So, what happens when your godly gang goes haywire?

It's the worry of most conscientious church leaders. This, more than anything else, makes them restrap every church function and instrument tightly to themselves. And the one-man band plays on.

Harmony can only return by retuning J.O.S.H.U.A. Check teamwork. Is everybody honestly contributing? Has a subgroup taken over? Who is the power-base? Redefine and debate teamwork. Check agreement on the overview: Are the goals agreed? By everybody? Do all acknowledge how their group is supposed to work?

Is sharing a reality? Is one, or more than one, holding back? Are people listening? Are honest thoughts fully shared? Have you as leader handled issues and circumstances appropriately? Is it the group or the leader at fault? It's usually six of one and half a dozen of the other.

In this case, would an outside, objective audit of the group help?

Are there any slackers? Is everybody trying their utmost? Who are the passengers? Does everybody feel appreciated?

If all else fails, the one-man band plays on. But do remember it is a novelty. Usually only clowns attempt it, and people are supposed to laugh at their output.

12

A Few Home Truths

Let's play Fantasy Soldiers again. Remember Seth and Dan querying just why they should be circumcised? That was Scene One. This now is . . .

SCENE TWO

In the background, priests ritualistically wield flint knives. Both SETH *and* DAN *wear pained expressions. The painful deed is done. They no longer strut like troopers. Rather, they tiptoe away with the grace of rheumatic ballet dancers.*

SETH: It's bad strategy!

DAN: What?

SETH: Attacking us rather than Jericho.

DAN: It's only a nick! For goodness sake, change the ram's horn, will you?

SETH [*grumbling half to himself*]: Messin' with knives when we should have been at 'em with swords. [*Now loudly.*] I say, we should 'ave marched straight out of the Jordan and right up to their front gate.

DAN: He knows what he's doing.

SETH: What's next? That's what I'd like to know.

DAN: Joshua works in mysterious ways.

SETH: But why?

DAN: God knows.

* * *

Do you ever wish you could switch on your very own *Question Time* with the Lord Almighty as the only panellist? We could all be questioning like Job in the Old Testament. Like him, we could grill the Lord on what he thought he was up to.

The Israelites too must have puzzled over some of God's decisions. They'd assembled on emerging from the Jordan basin. Jericho was a stone's throw away. Now they had to take a three-day break in their Gilgal holiday camp.

'Certainly it must [have been] the right moment to launch an all-out offensive,' writes Alan Redpath as he skilfully deals with the Hebrew delay at Gilgal.

> 'But no, God is never in a hurry. God's delays are always more profitable than our haste. We are always in a fever to do something for God and have forgotten that the first thing God wants is that we should *be* something for him. In this time of delay God had lessons to teach his people which were going to decide all the future course of warfare in the land.'[1]

The Israelites needed to know a few home truths as they entered their new home. A quiet time was needed to catch the vision and pass it on. It also helped them to reflect on how they were going to manage in the future.

More than this, they had to realise that the Jordan represented a clean break from the rebellious past. The river was a symbolic cleansing. They needed to sparkle as the holy people of God. It was followed by repentance for their disobedience – undoubtedly part of the circumcision ritual. Confession. A fresh start. Firmly restored to God's forgiving arms.

Their confession must have been something to hear. As a nation, they had rebelled against God's global salvation plan. There had been the refusal to go into the Promised Land, not to mention the worship of false gods and a golden calf at the foot of Mount Sinai (Ex 32). Perhaps there had even been sacrifices of children to Molech.

A lot to confess

The Israelites' family portrait gallery was a litany of tut-tuts. It went all the way back to Abraham's nephew Lot.

Lot himself was a salt-of-the-earth type. So too was his wife, though in a different way. She turned her back on God's future by the Dead Sea and was petrified into a pillar of the stuff.

Her two girls dodged the salt, but followed in Mum's wayward footsteps in other ways.

There were no marriageable chaps around, so Miss Lot the Elder told Miss Lot the Younger that the only way to carry on the family line was to get Dad drunk and seduce him (Gen 19:30–38).

'I'll do it the first night and you do it the second' is an abbreviated form of their agreement.

Generations later, Moses and Joshua could hardly move in the wilderness without bumping into the immoral consequences of those two nights. Lottie the Elder produced Moab who begat the Moabites. Lottie Junior produced Ben-ammi, whose son Ammi begat the Ammonites.

Joshua's lot was not a happy one largely due to several lifetimes of rebellion and sin from a wayward people. But now the Jordan and Gilgal was a break from the past, and a new start.

At least, that was the plan.

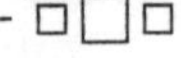

A nation repents

We can only guess at what national repentance might involve, never having done it ourselves. But let's have a go. After all, one nation's sin is very much like any other's, especially when that nation exists as though God doesn't. Israel ignored their Creator for part of their wilderness years. Many suggest Britain has been doing it for a lot longer.

We're not very good at national repentance. The closest we have managed is 'a careful self-analysis of what's going wrong with society' when two boys kill a toddler. There was also the time newspapers said they were sorry for the death of a princess. But apart from this, we are unskilled in repentance. However, let's try our best. It will help us understand what Gilgal must have meant to the Israelites.

Our confession might go something like this:

We repent of . . .

- Half the population owning 93 per cent of the nation's wealth while the other half share out 7 per cent;
- The highest divorce rate in Europe;
- Soaring crime figures, with half of all young women afraid to go out at night;
- Bad parenting (pre-teen kids commit 30,000 crimes a year. A third of junior criminals are girls);
- 177,000 pre-birth babies killed annually;
- One in four couples living together without the commitment of marriage;
- One in three babies born out of wedlock;
- Teenagers believing they're abnormal if still virgins;
- Bishops accepting homosexuality among laity, and a nation which thinks gay sex is normal.

It's probably a good job God doesn't need Britain to play the starring role in his global drama of salvation. We seem more suited for the alternative scene. The ape of God – as the devil is called – might give us the title role in his version.

Unless, that is, a miracle happened, as it must have done with Israel.

Can you imagine Britain having its own Gilgal? Every event stadium in Britain would be packed to capacity with millions. All kneeling. On huge live-link video screens, Archbishop Joshua of Canterbury would lead the nation to repentance. As the confession ends, each man is called to the front to stand before the screen for circumcision.

Difficult to imagine it happening at Wembley.

But it happened at Gilgal.

No wonder Israel felt renewed and cleansed before God. That's why they could take on just about anybody with anything. They could even go to war on a fortified city with trumpets. Each of us knows how good we feel when we get right with God. When three million people feel like that at the same time and in the same place . . . world, watch out!

Envisioned. Renewed. Repentant. Ready for action. Anyone for Jericho? Joshua was.

But hold on. There's more to sow in the minds of the Israelites, and even in Joshua. God's got more to teach at the Spring Harvest of Gilgal.

Halt! Who goes there?

Old habits die hard. Joshua, just before the big push, couldn't resist a little spying mission of his own. Unexpectedly, it was to land him flat on his face.

As he neared the city, he met a man with a drawn sword in his hand.

'Friend or foe?' Joshua challenged.

'No!' came the reply, and before our man could hint that the reply wasn't exactly helpful, the swordsman added, 'But as the commander of the army of the Lord I have now come.'

Two commanders of the Lord's army?

Face to face?

Well, not quite face to face. Joshua had already hit the ground. His mind had quickly worked out what was happening. Alas, we are still left wondering. The identity of the commander of the Lord's army is not revealed to us, though many have speculated.

We are also left to wrestle with its meaning.

Commander of the Lord's army

This commander could have been God himself in human form (a theophany). He did the same with Adam and Eve in the garden (Gen 3:8) and with Abraham (Gen 18:1). Jacob, after an all-night wrestling match with a similarly mysterious figure, cried out, 'I saw God face to face' (Gen 32:30).

If Joshua's commander was not God, then possibly it was an angelic visitation. If so, it could have been the archangel Michael, who certainly commands the Lord's army at the end of time. In Revelation he leads war against Satan or the dragon (Rev 12:7).

After these and other considerations, it is best to be reverently agnostic. We would be foolish to define that which God leaves out of focus.

Reassurance?

The appearance of the heavenly commander could have been confirmation to Joshua that the Lord really was with him as he prepared for the first major battle for Canaan. If so, this is beautiful. An almighty God caring enough to, yet again, give his servant awesome reassurance. He did it to Moses through a burning bush, and now this time for Joshua. Even the same burning bush words are used: 'Take off your sandals, for the place where you are standing is holy' (Josh 5; 15; Ex 3:5). And Joshua did. This version is certainly in character with a God who comes to meet us where we most need him.

Watch it!

But perhaps there was one more reason for the special appearance. Maybe it was to keep Joshua's feet firmly on the ground. Miracles are heady stuff. Remember that time when you felt God had worked through you. Maybe it was a healing prayer, or a word of wisdom into a difficult situation. Perhaps you had delivered a first-rate sermon, or Sunday school class. In Joshua's case, it was holding up a mighty river while three million crossed over.

I don't know how you felt afterwards. As for me, there is always a mixture of emotions: humility at being used, delight at helping somebody and sheer relief that it worked. But – human motives are never without a but – lurking somewhere under all that, there was a grain of pride. Soon, it grows to crumb-size. Then a slice . . . .

'I did it . . . well, no, not I, but God, you understand . . . . Yes, praise the Lord. He actually used me. *Me*! My goodness! I must be somebody special. *No*! I mean, of course, that the Lord uses anybody, even an ass at one point of the Old Testament. Still . . . well . . . maybe, just possibly I am a bit special . . . . I mean, he doesn't just use any Tom, Dick or Harry, you know, and . . . .'

God doesn't use many of us for miracles. We can't cope. He can't trust us. We can't trust ourselves. And maybe, just maybe, the commander of the Lord's army was reminding Joshua just who was in charge.

Marching silent

Whatever the Lord had in mind for Joshua, one thing comes over loud and clear: the battle orders. 'March a silent army of 40,000 around Jericho once each day. Seven priests are to blow rams' horns in front of the ark [a brisk march around Jericho outside arrow range took me about half an hour]. On the seventh day, do seven laps, silent except for the trumpeting priests. Then give a loud shout and the city wall will fall. Everything is to be sacrificed to the Lord, save for Rahab and her family, for she helped my spies to escape. Her faith has saved her and them' (see Joshua 6).

During the next week they carried out these instructions to the letter – and the wall came tumbling down.

How?

Again, modern man demands some rationale for miracles, so let's humour him for a moment.

Some commentators believe it was an earthquake. No, say others. It was the noise. Our dog's bark can make the doorbell ring. Opera sopranos can shatter glasses. What would 40,000 shouts do? With houses built on walls, which themselves sat on the walls of previous settlements, who knows?

Again, my inclination is to steer away from rational explanations. I just want to tell modern man to adopt the insurance policy approach: accept them as acts of God. The more we try to find the natural in the supernatural, the harder it will be when we come up against an act of God that defies all human ingenuity. I have in mind the resurrection, the incarnation and the virgin birth. And just one more: the day the sun stood still.

While we're sitting with our feet up in Gilgal, let me jump ahead to that day.

Wanted: childlike faith

The longer you stay in Joshua's company the more you want to hum that children's action chorus, *My God is so big, so strong and so mighty, there's nothing my God cannot do*. He's mind-stretching. Faith-inflating.

Looking at the Joshua events demands the same childlike faith that he had. The same childlike faith that his New Testament namesake was to demand for entry into the kingdom of God. Unless we become 'like children . . . ' (Lk 18:17).

Childlike, not childish.

Childish faith is immature, unreasonable and blind. Childlike faith is walking through the Exodus sea because you've already seen God do mightier things in Egypt.

Childlike faith is my son and daughter, when toddlers, launching themselves from the top of the stairs shouting 'Catch me, Daddy,' because I had never let them drop before.

Childlike faith is walking round a city blowing your trumpet while thousands of Jerichonians fall about the ramparts in hysterics. It is believing that, sadly, they won't have the last laugh on the seventh day.

Childlike faith is knowing that God will do what he says because he has done it in the past.

Childlike faith on the day the sun stood still was marching against five kings at the head of the biggest army you've yet faced. It was going up against them despite having yomped many miles through the night. You have to act quickly for you have neither the supply lines nor energy reserves for a long campaign. If you don't win that day, you will have to retreat in humiliation.

Yet, you march on to the battlefield knowing that you're going to need more than a day to finish off such a mighty army. Humanly speaking, you will not win. Army strategists tell you it'll be a miracle if you even hold your own. Nobody gives you a chance. But you know that you're under God's orders, just as you were at the River Jordan. He didn't let you down then. Nor will he now. Somehow, some way, your God will make it happen.

He'll do it even if he has to make the sun stand still to give you more fighting time.

Now that is childlike faith. That is trusting God.

They were not required to bury their brains and gormlessly suck their thumbs. This was no blind leap into battle. This was going through the trust barrier. It is only when we step through faith that God's safe arms catch us.

Sometimes, sadly, we never launch ourselves into his arms. We don't dare give him a chance.

Miracles don't come much bigger

So, the sun stops. And the moon. More likely, it was the earth that stood still. Whatever, absolute chaos would naturally follow. If the earth stood still, by natural law the battle should have finished there and then – all of the participants squashed to pulp. Our pleasant existence is only assured because gravity keeps our feet on the ground while the outward force of a spinning planet stops our heads joining them. That's what Isaac Newton said, anyway.

As you read this, you're in a solar system travelling at 45,000 miles per hour towards the constellation of Hercules. At the same time, in a different plane, you are speeding at 66,000 miles per hour around the sun. Yet again, we are rotating on the earth's axis every 23 hours and 56.41 minutes. Now, I don't know where you are reading this in relationship to the equator, but I'm typing this in the north of England. As I do so I'm 'orbiting' at just below the sound barrier.

Meanwhile, back in the Promised Land, Joshua and the armies were nearer to the equator. They would be at well over Mach One.

Then Joshua said, '"O sun, stand still over Gibeon, O moon over the Valley of Aijalon." So the sun stood still, and the moon stopped, till the nation avenged itself on its enemies' (Josh 10:12–13). And the Lord made it so.

Why should we accept this story today when we know how impossible it is?

Answers: Because God made motion. Because he created speed. It was his hands that placed the stars and suns and planets in their paths. Because he is the boss, and gravity isn't. Nor any other astronomical force. Not the earth, nor the sun, nor the moon. We can believe this story because childlike trust knows that he created the universe and all its forces, and therefore we can trust him. Joshua did.

I juggle, as I mentioned before. If a puny being can keep five balls going at once (the world record is upwards of eleven), then I am quite sure that God can manage a billion galaxies through his beautifully precise laws.

I never ever want to have to stand up in church and sing, *My god is so weak, so wet and so puny, most everything god cannot do.*

People's problems with miracles lie not in the miracles. Their problem lies in their god. A God big enough for a capital 'G' has miracles for breakfast. They're the most natural thing in his world.

A liberal miracle

You've heard the one about the liberal who preached that an east wind blew away the Exodus sea so that the Hebrews paddled over in a couple of inches of water. On hearing this, an elderly Pentecostal lady leaped into the air and shouted, 'Hallelujah! What a miracle!'

'Pardon?' queried the liberal preacher.

'Until this moment, I'd never seen how great God really is!' she shouted back. 'Fancy drowning the whole Egyptian army in just two inches of water!'

The liberal who insists that God isn't into magic tricks and miracles has a further problem.

A miracle, so states one dictionary, is 'an event that so overrides what observers understand of natural law that it creates wonder and serves as evidence of God's intervention in this universe'.[2]

The natural law of God is to love; to bear our burdens; to forgive us; to die for us. It is therefore natural for God to want to get involved with us. The natural law of God is that he will intervene to save us and help us.

It would indeed be a miracle of great magnitude if this natural law was suspended and God didn't get involved.

The how of the sun standing still is not as important as the happening. The same is true for the walls of Jericho. And through them God was still teaching Joshua and his people. He even used a prostitute to show what true faith is . . . .

Notes

1 Alan Redpath, *Victorious Christian Living*, p 77.
2 Laurence Richards (ed.), *The Applied Bible Dictionary* (Kingsway, 1990), p 670.

13
God Loves Prostitutes

A video dropped out of the wrapping paper. The House of Cyn *was its title, sent by a former high society madam called Cynthia. She had signed it, and added mischievously, 'Thank you for past custom!'*

With it came an invitation to one of her respectable parties with an accompanying note, 'Bring Linda along, if you'll feel safer.'

'Lord, keep working,' my wife and I pray. 'She'll make a marvellous Christian with her knack of hospitality.'

At one time, she wanted to open up a 'House of Cyn' pub in our town. We had stood against her plans at the licensing magistrates. She didn't get her house but, unexpectedly, we got a friend, despite our opposition. In turn, she got two friends.

Ten years ago, I might not have even spoken to her, but then Spring Harvest speaker Tony Campolo hadn't made me see Jesus and the forgiven prostitute in a true light.

He tells the story of a group of call girls in an all-night bus depot café. One is crying. He himself was returning home from a 'preach' and observed the sadness as he waited for his connection. It turned out that the tears were for a birthday that nobody had remembered.

'And there's nobody who would remember either,' sobbed the girl.

'Say,' Campolo drawled to the Italian café owner after the girls had returned to the streets, 'let's do something for their next coffee break. My bus isn't until the early hours. At least we could get her a cake.'

'I get a-busy with the cake,' called through the owner's wife having overheard the suggestion. 'You men-a do some trimmings and things.'

At 3.30 am the girls' return was greeted with a small procession, singing appropriate birthday greetings, and bearing an iced cake topped by a single lighted candle. The birthday girl was stunned to silence. Tears brimmed.

'Come on, Elsie,' shouted the café owner self-consciously. 'Happy birffday! Now, getta da cake cut.'

She was handed the knife and they waited. And waited. Elsie stood rooted in her fishnets and high heels. Face muscles twitched and stifled.

'Hey, babe!' exclaimed the owner once more. 'I gotta business to run. Please, cutta da cake!'

'No!' It came with a half sob and Elsie turned to Tony Campolo. 'Hey, mister. Please don't let them make me cut the cake. You can have all the rest of the party stuff but, please, let me take the cake home.'

'Of course,' he said. 'But why?'

'Nobody ever did anything like this for me before, mister,' sobbed Elsie. 'I just wanna take it home and keep it. Can I? Please?'

At this point in the story, Tony Campolo yelled across the Spring Harvest big top tent over 5,000 heads, 'I wanna belong to a church that throws parties for prostitutes!'

* * *

Good words to consider. But now, meditate on the following sentences. Joshua had to (Josh 1:8).

> If a priest's daughter defiles herself by becoming a prostitute, she disgraces her father; she must be burned in the fire (Lev 21:9).

> If, however, the charge is true and no proof of the girl's virginity can be found, she shall be brought to the door of her father's house and there the men of her town shall stone her to death (Deut 22:20–21).

Consider now what Joshua did on encountering his first prostitute in the Promised Land. It came in a report from his two spies. They had been harboured in Jericho by the prostitute Rahab, who had then helped them to escape. The spies had in turn promised Rahab safety.

'Go into the prostitute's house,' he told the two men as the attack was launched, 'and bring her out and all who belong to her . . . ' (Josh 6:22).

Joshua spared Rahab and her family, and her story reveals so much about her saviour, our God and ourselves.

As far as the corruption of Canaan was concerned, Joshua was the executioner of a God who had run out of patience with a nation whose sinning days were over. Yet, even as the blood-letting was about to begin, Joshua was moved to show mercy. Certainly, there was to be no compassion for any Israelites who might have turned their tents into brothels. There was judgement for those who sinned without thought for the damage it would wreak in God's holy people. But for those like Rahab who believed in God, who feared God, there was forgiveness and another chance.

Joshua's saving action was to put a prostitute on the road to sainthood, as we shall soon see.

Joshua himself knew a God of the second chance. He himself was forgiven. So why not a madam? There was consequently nobody Joshua and God would not forgive.

And as I write I'm challenged: who wouldn't I love enough to forgive? Child molesters? Paedophiles? Rapists?

Wife beaters? Doubting bishops? Disloyal priests? Not, of course, that my forgiveness counts, only for my own spiritual well-being. We have to agree with Joshua that there is, in fact, no individual or group beyond our love for, amazingly, not one of us is beyond God's love.

And certainly not a prostitute who lived in Jericho. Her story opens up not only more of Joshua's character, but also his first major Promised Land challenge.

With a little judicious use of imagination, the prostitute's tale might have gone something like this . . . .

* * *

What's a girl to do? Starving. Hard-up. Not knowing whether you'll eat today or even this week.

Before, as a temple prostitute, life had been comfortable. Then she had peaked. She had declined below Baal's divine standards, according to local priests. Her days acting as a stand-in goddess in the national spiritual health service were well over. Only private practice was now left to her. Yet, she still had a figure and face of some attraction. Rahab still made heads turn despite the down-at-heel sandals and hair tangled with sand and grit.

She would just have to cope with the self-righteous Jerichonians. They now threw stones at her rather than their bodies. Most of the time she could easily avoid them. She was one of the Outer Wallers, the flotsam of a society, who couldn't afford the safe suburbs of the inner town. All that was left to her was the least wanted, most dangerous place in Jericho. It was a room on the city parapets. The view was great, though not when arrows and siege boulders crashed through the window. In Jericho that was often. It was a city in great demand by a host of foreign forces.

Walls of Jericho

Rahab's house formed part of the city wall. It wasn't at ground floor level. In fact, it must have been quite high up because the two spies had to be let down by rope from her window (Josh 2:15).

Archaeologists have shown that the city was surrounded by two walls, in places as high as 30ft. The inner wall was up to 12ft thick with the outer wall being half that width. The distance between the walls varied between 12 and 27 feet. Rahab's 'flat', like many others, probably straddled the two walls at a narrow point.

Jericho, as noted already, was not big by modern standards. It would have fitted into Wembley Stadium with ease. Town-house prices must have been sky-high due to shortage of building land. They would have had little alternative but to convert the walls into living accommodation, and the town planners would not have objected. It might have been dangerous for the occupants, but it would have provided extra security for the inner-city dwellers.

Nobody these days gave Rahab much, except for violence and sex, and perhaps a few shekels for family support. It was to be several hundred years before somebody would stand up for the likes of her against the prigs of propriety. How often must she have yearned for a kind voice. She would have loved the protection of this simple sentence: 'Let him who is without sin cast the first stone' (see John 8:7).

She would have been shocked to the core had she realised that such a champion was going to be her great, great grandson several times removed.

Incredible to think that God chose a prostitute to be an ancestor of his one and only Son. Incredible to think that God loves prostitutes that much. No wonder Jesus, when he arrived, was a friend of sinners. Rahab was the mother of his ancestors; she was great grandmother of King David who was himself a murderer and adulterer.

God may hate the sin. But you can't accuse him ever of hating sinners. They're in the family.

Joshua saved Rahab because he recognised another truth: God would use anybody, even Rahab. And also himself. The lowest and the highest. Those in between. Anybody. You and me. But more. God will use anybody so long as they want to be used. So long as they hunger for it.

Joshua was certainly ready to be used after seeing the hell of Canaan and capturing the vision of what God wanted to do. Certainly he had fears. But he wanted to be used.

Rahab wanted it as well, for different reasons. Having heard of the greatness of this new God – greater than Baal, El, Astarte, greater even than the child-thirsty Molech – she wanted to be on his side. She also wanted safety for her family.

'I know that the Lord has given this land to you and that a great fear of you has fallen on us . . . ' she told the two spies whom she hid on the roof of her brothel. 'We have heard how the Lord dried up the water of the Red Sea . . . and what you did to Sihon and Og . . . our hearts sank and everyone's courage failed because of you . . . . Now then, please swear to me by the Lord that you will show kindness to my family, because I have shown kindness to you' (Josh 2:9–12).

Sihon and Og

King Sihon's Amorite realm was on the east bank of the Jordan. In the early days of the wilderness wanderings Israel needed permission to pass through. Despite assurances that they would be ideal tourists, Sihon refused them visas. Further, he marched out with his threatening army. Moses was left with little alternative but to defend himself.

The same thing happened with Sihon's brother Og, king

of neighbouring Bashan. In the process, Moses put both kings to the sword and destroyed their cities.

So swift and successful were these battles that poets scribbled furiously on parchment, pots, clay tablets, in fact anything they could lay their hands on. Soon Israel's tough reputation was widespread.

She desperately wanted to be used by this great God. And, yes, it was out of fear. It was also out of faith. This prostitute's trust was so superb that she made the pages of the biblical equivalent of *The Guinness Book of Records* in Hebrews chapter 11.

'Now faith,' states the writer of Hebrews, 'is being sure of what we hope for and certain of what we do not see.' Just like those in the ancient gallery of greats – Abel, Enoch, Noah, Abraham, Isaac and Jacob, Moses and, yes, the prostitute Rahab.

The Guinness Book of Records is updated and reprinted each year. God's records of his superlative servants are adjusted every time you and I step out in faith. Like Rahab. Like Joshua. Like you. Imagine hearing your name read at the end of time in the updated version of Hebrews chapter 11.

Of course, standing up for God will make you stand out from your crowd. It did for Joshua, that time he was threatened with stoning. It surely did for Rahab.

The Jericho crowd had its egg-head intellectuals. No doubt there were sceptics too, though probably not many. Mostly, they were into the occult and magic with their nature god Baal. They too had their Mystic Megs, horoscopes, mediums, X-files and UFOs, fortune-telling and tarot cards. And Rahab was called to stand out against the prevailing beliefs and stand up for this new and almighty God. She did. And, true, her motives were by no means pure. She saved the spies so that they might save her and her family. But God again is amazing. He takes all-comers, regardless of initial motives. Then, he immerses their fears in his gifts of security. He acts first, so that we might act in response.

In summary so far, Joshua's first stronghold in the new land was to be gained through a prostitute. He will surely use you and me. We are called to love sinners, for we are of the same stock. There, but for the grace of God . . . . Those who want to be used by God need only to show their hunger and faith. God will use us in spite of our initial motives and fears.

The superheroes of Scripture are only ordinary men and women who took a step of faith. For them – hiding spies under flax on a flat roof, or stepping into a running river – it was a small step, powered by God. To the rest of mankind they seem like giant leaps.

Joshua and Rahab show that anybody, with God's impetus, can do the same. Even fighting a major battle armed only with the instruments of the regimental brass band.

Thanks to Rahab, the attack on Jericho happened just as God ordered it.

Well not exactly.

A man called Achan decided that one or two rather expensive items should be sacrificed to Achan rather than the Lord. It was going to cost him his life. More. It would bring Israel her first home defeat.

14
Beware Success!

Nothing fails quite so spectacularly as a huge success.

Jericho, for instance, may have changed hands often, but the city that stood in Joshua's time had endured for generations. The king and citizens were justly proud of their winning ways and walls. Then came the sensational collapse.

Over the rubble of that failure, the Israelites scrambled to their success. It was giant-killing. Fourth division Flint Aged nomads versus premier Bronze Age prosperity. So great was it that the victors flopped the next time out. Israel and Joshua thought they knew it all. So confident were they that they locked out their manager.

'Who needs him?' they thought.

Their next opponents were non-league and couldn't even afford a consonant – Ai. Besides that, it wasn't exactly a name to inspire – 'The Heap'! It had few men and Joshua's scouts reported that Ai didn't have a prayer.

'In that case,' Joshua's actions seemed to say, 'I don't need one either. Why bother the Almighty over trivia? We can't fail. We've arrived.'

A town like Ai

'Bible is proved wrong!'

That was an over-the-top headline when the results of two short digs at Ai were reported in the thirties.

They were the findings of Mme Judith Marquet-Krause, as reported after her untimely death by M. Dussard. A triple-walled prosperous city destroyed in about 2200 BC was unearthed, plus a small Hebrew village of about 1100 BC. Digs there showed nothing of a settlement around 1400 BC when Jericho was attacked.

What the newspapers failed to report were the earlier test diggings of Professor Garstang and Dr Albright. They concluded that there could have been a settlement in Joshua's day. The papers also failed to note that Mme Marquet-Krause had nowhere near finished her archaeological work at Ai before her early death.

Another theory suggests that Ai was probably little more than a few wooden fortifications and mud huts. It was manned only by a platoon of men from both Ai and nearby Bethel, hence the spies finding only a few troops. As with Jericho, the mass of the population would have been spread around the lush farming region.

If this theory is correct, it would account for archaeologists finding next to nothing at Ai for the Joshua period.

Another theory suggests that we have yet to find the true location of the biblical Ai.

Joshua seemed to view success as a plateau gained rather than an Everest on which to balance. He forgot that summits have a shortage of 'ups' and an excess of 'downs', and are generally not designed for long stays.

However, to be fair to Israel, when they were up, they really were up – an impressive model for all who seek the premier spiritual life.

Discipline

Forty thousand marched round Jericho with not a word. Just seven trumpets blowing. Imagine your church moving with such unity. Picture all church council leaders or deacons gagged by God, even the vicar! Miracles happen in any age. Nobody murmured. All disciplined warriors of God, marching as to war.

Obedience

A daily half-hour trek around the city and back to their tents each time, just as the Lord commanded. No one urged attack, despite the waves of fear radiating from a terrified city. Apparent success or fear of failure are the chief causes of Christian disobedience. The first makes us run faster than we should. The last makes us run away.

Steadfastness

They persevered with the plan. Nobody rolled out the weapons for city siege. They stuck with their rams' horns and silent marches, and followed the ark. The clarion of trumpets gave them the solemnity of religious ritual. The ark declared that God was in his place, and all was well.

God's number

Numbers in Scripture often have special significance. Six, for instance, is the human number. We were made on the sixth day, and given six days to work. A Hebrew slave had to serve six years to be a free man. The number associated with God is seven. The man who seeks to be God ends up as 666 recurring – the mark of a beast who never quite made it.

God's number abounds around Jericho. The Hebrews would have recognised it and loved it. There were seven priests, seven rams' horns and seven days. On the seventh day they marched round before shouting at the end of the seventh lap.

For the Hebrew it shouted out: this is God's doing, and he is with us.

□□□

Faith

On the final day, thousands of men, up in arms for a holy cause, shouted at the top of their voices trusting in God to keep his word. He did, and the walls came tumbling down. It must have been awe-inspiring. The ranks were 100 per cent dedicated to God, with 99.9 per cent of them devoting everything to him.

Pity about the 0.1 per cent – Achan. There's always one, isn't there?

This body of God's men – disciplined, obedient, steadfast and faithful – was shot through with Achanitis. Diagnosis of this disease is easy for observers. Self-diagnosis, though, can be a problem. The eyes are green with envy and there are yellow streaks of cowardly treachery. During the sacking of Jericho, Achan beheld a beautiful Babylonian robe, a gold ingot as heavy as a brick and some silver. He knew full well that this first city of the Promised Land was promised entirely to the Lord, but after forty years in the wilderness, the temptation was too much. He took the treasure and buried it in the floor of his tent (Josh 7:20–21).

Two things now put Israel's success in double jeopardy – the deafness of Joshua and the desires of Achan.

The deafness of Joshua

'What now, Lord?'

Just such a simple question would have ensured Israel's continuing success. God could have quietly whispered that

Achan needed to be disciplined before his example spread from family to clan, to tribe and nation.

But then the spies returned from Ai. Joshua listened to them instead of God. He dispatched a small company for what would surely be a fringe skirmish.

In this situation, what was God to do? Turn a blind eye? Overlook the ravages of Achanitis and egoitis on his body? Should he conclude, 'Well, they've done well so far. And, after all, Achan and family are only a tiny percentage of the whole. And Joshua has had a difficult few days. Perhaps, just for once, I'll go easy on them'?

A goodish and moderately holy God might have said that. In that case, Israel would have been the ideal signpost to point the rest of the world to such a shop-soiled deity. Israel, however, were in no shape to represent a totally holy and utterly perfect God. Their lifestyle broke at least two of the commandments. They created a false image of the Life-giver. They took God's name in vain – claiming to be his people yet not behaving like it.

If only they would just stop long enough to listen. If only they would recall two of the primary keys to spiritual success – going to God's word and hearing rightly, and listening to God in prayer.

But how was the Lord to get their attention?

In the wilderness years, he had time to be gentle. He could nudge his beloved towards him by giving them their daily bread. He could guide them by day with a pillar of cloud and by night with a pillar of fire (Ex 13:21–22). For more rebellious times, a tougher line was taken, with various punishments (in the Book of Leviticus) graded to fit their crimes.

But now they were at war.

Joshua and Israel had gone absent without leave. The deserters were doing their own thing, and one family was in open rebellion. This was no time for nudges. War demands warlike penalties. There was no other alternative but that God use the enemy to bring his people back to their senses.

'So about three thousand men went up; but they were routed by the men of Ai, who killed about thirty-six of them . . . . At this the hearts of the people melted and became like water' (Josh 7:4–5).

The desired effect was achieved.

'Then Joshua tore his clothes and fell face down to the ground before the ark of the Lord, remaining there till evening. The elders of Israel did the same, and sprinkled dust on their heads' (Josh 7:6).

Clothes-tearing

Joshua may have suffered from divine deafness but he did get one thing right. On hearing of the thirty-six deaths at Ai, he followed divinely authorised forms of mourning by tearing his clothes and sprinkling dust on his head. He could also have let his hair down (unbraided long hair) and wept (Lev 21:1–4).

This was new to Canaan. Previously, the residents went in for 'rounding' the corners of the head (some sort of self-mutilation), cutting their flesh and offering tithes to the dead.

It's good to compare and contrast our God with his pagan rivals. Thank God that he is no cruel deity demanding satisfaction through human blood-letting (Deut 26:14).

Now God had Israel's full and undivided attention, even though they were somewhat annoyed. In Joshua's indignant words, 'Why did you ever bring this people across the Jordan to deliver us into the hands of the Amorites to destroy us?' (Josh 7:7).

But eventually Joshua asked that vital question which

should have been asked on the successful summit of Jericho: 'What then will you do?'

Now he was ready to hear. Spiritual deafness was receding.

The key to godly success is listening, but not just to anybody. Not only to self. Not exclusively to experts and spies, no matter how knowledgeable. Listen to Father. The key to success is useless when it is not in the right lock.

Had Joshua keyed in to God at Jericho, thirty-six of his soldiers would not have died. He would still be the hero of the hour and the hearts of Israel would not have 'melted' and become 'like water' (Josh 7:5). Instead, they would have been ice-cool in Ai.

But stop!

Before we go any further, Joshua is not really the villain of this piece.

Let the main culprit be brought to book – Achan.

15
The Stoning

Ai had fallen. Thirty-six troopers lay dead. Who was to blame for God's wrath?

To discover this, Joshua held a divine elimination contest. Tribes and clans and families were paraded before the Lord (Josh 7:16ff). The lot eventually fell upon Achan.

The national lot

It's not clear if the tribes, clans, families and finally Achan were singled out by Israel's version of the national lottery.

Rather than forty-nine numbered balls, they used two flat pebbles, which were kept in the breastplate of the high priest. One side of each was called the Urim ('to curse'), while the positive side was called the Thummim ('to be perfect'). If a toss of the pebbles produced two Urims – a double negative – that was a definite thumbs-down.

This was possibly how Joshua knew which group to single out, all the way down to Achan and his family. The lot fell on God's choice. Joshua certainly used the national 'allottery' later to divide up the land between the tribes (Josh 14:1–2).

By the way, this is not the green light for a lottery

flutter next Saturday. The Israelites believed that God was the power of the universe, so it was nothing to adjust gravity so that the Urim and Thummim landed in line with his will.

David Pawson gives an excellent description of this in his Joshua tapes, from where I borrowed his national lottery idea.

'If God can pull down the walls of Jericho,' he explains, 'he can certainly determine lots . . . they used lots deliberately so that man had no influence . . . they used lots right up to the day of Pentecost . . . (and the lot fell on Matthias) . . . after that, God's Spirit guided them (and lotteries were no longer needed).'

The desires of Achan

'Tell me what you have done,' said Joshua. 'Do not hide it from me.'

'It is true!' cried Achan. 'I have sinned against the Lord, the God of Israel. This is what I have done . . . .'

After the confession, Joshua added his stern judgement.

'Why have you brought this trouble on us? The Lord will bring trouble on you today.'

The Israelites took Achan and all his family to a nearby valley and stoned them to death before burning them. They called it the Valley of Trouble (Achor).

Stoned them!

Burned them!

It takes a modern man's breath away.

And God told them to do it. . . .

The death penalty for a fancy robe and a fistful of gold and silver. Not even a decent spell on death row. No appeal. No civilised lethal injection. Immediate execution by stoning! What sort of man is this Joshua? And his God? Mashing human beings into bloody pulps?

Round our way, the local magistrates would have given Achan a suspended sentence and a 120-hour community service order. The only way he and his family would have got stoned was celebrating their freedom in the pub afterwards.

What are we to make of this discrepancy between ancient and modern approaches to justice?

I believe the first cause of it is today's . . . .

Poor view of sin

Many in our liberal age throw away the word SIN except for the initial 's'. They then add other letters to redefine it for our refined society: sickness . . . social deprivation . . . Saturday night fever . . . schizoid . . . self-fulfilment . . . self-interest . . . self-righteous . . . self-satisfied . . . self-willed. Anything but sin.

Not only do we play down sin, but we scale down the consequences of it.

Our church helped to set up a community association, and something about my person made me the unanimous choice for Chairman of Rubbish. We've had spring-cleans, anti-litter posters, school essay competitions. We've even sent a nice 'bin-it-or-else' letter to each resident. Despite all this, the community and the local rubbish dump are still one and the same. And for one simple reason, according to our local newsagent Alf. Astonishingly, nobody in the history of our town has ever been charged with a litter offence.

Proposition: fine three litter louts in three consecutive weeks £200 a piece. Result: our streets and our rubbish will soon part company. Official action taken so far: 'Well, let's see if something turns up, shall we?'

A society that is easy on sin, whatever it is, will sin with ease. Only when it takes sin seriously will it stand a chance.

Once it writes SIN big and recognises the big selfish 'I' in the middle of the nasty little word, remedies become a possibility. Should it then start to make the punishment fit the crime of the selfish 'I', then it can start to hope. And still one more step. If it ever reaches general agreement on what or who judges sin, it may very well be on to a winner.

Israel had all the ingredients for law and order in their book of by-laws left by Moses. Sin was spelled out in detail. The consequences and punishments – from a fine to execution – were plainly set out. The rule against which to test actions was the Ten Commandments.

Israel had one further advantage. The family album of bad characters revealed precisely how a holy God reacted against sin. The rogues' gallery included murderer Cain, that Dead Sea lot in Sodom and Gomorrah, Dreamcoat Joseph's jealous brothers. Then there were the 3,000 golden calf heretics who were swallowed up at the foot of Mount Sinai.

The black sheep of the family were good for one thing only: they kept the rest of the flock in check.

Achan was brought up in this strict, yet fair, society. He was executed because he knowingly placed the whole nation at risk from the consequences of God's law. Further, he was responsible for the deaths of thirty-six fellow Israelites, not to mention national humiliation and defeat. His sin was nothing short of treason, and even in sophisticated England, traitors can still be hanged. At least there are some similarities between God's view of sin and today's view.

Hell-bound

There is a second reason why moderns struggle with Achan's stoning.

They fail to see what the Lord sees – his beloved world plunging at the speed of light into the darkness of hell. There was just a chance that the man's poor view of sin might be improved by catching a view of men and women behaving in a godly way.

Sinless, Israel never was

A godly Israel, even a sinless one, was to be an excellent example to the rest of humanity. The idea, of course, was doomed to failure, human nature being what it is.

Yet, God must have known this. So, what was he really up to when he erected this faulty signpost at the world's crossroads?

The simple answer is: It was one of many lessons for a world that only learned the hard way.

I once wrote a novel. The first three chapters were better than Dickens. Masterclass! The trouble was, only I could see this obvious truth. 'Over the top,' was my wife's verdict. My daughter desecrated the chapters with cruel red ink. One test reader thought I'd swallowed a thesaurus. Two suggested I shouldn't give up my day job. But I only got the message when a friendly publisher commented, 'You write as though you are trying to convince everybody that you're a novelist.'

As far as education of self is concerned, I gather one or two other humans are like me. Lessons have to be applied with a sledgehammer. We only learn the hard way.

The Old Testament is about God pursuing a relationship with his people, while his people ignore him and pursue just about everything and everybody else. And they rarely learn.

The sad day humanity fell, God dropped in to evict them from his garden, but promised he would eventually send them down a Saviour.

But they didn't listen. Not even after the Flood. Not even when they got Ten Commandments to teach them right and wrong.

The Old Testament gives one illustration after another

– prophet after prophet – to show that, no matter how much a loving God tries to ease the lot of humanity, we learn only after the hardest lessons.

Sadly, some don't even learn then. Not even when they are given a homeland, a rule book and the personal attention of a God who promised to be with them.

Humanity had to learn that there was no way they would ever be able to save themselves. What they needed was a totally new thing from the Lord. A new covenant. A new way of salvation that didn't rely on them keeping the law.

They needed to learn the hard way that they needed a Saviour.

The sleaze of the Achan affair marred such a vision.

And lest you think this form of divine judgement went out with the Old Testament, remember that a similar scenario happened 1,400 years later when God's Son set up his new people. This time it was another 'A' – Ananias. He and his wife, Sapphira, did an Achan by dishonestly declaring that they had devoted property to God which they hadn't. They, like Achan, were struck down dead. Such treachery against God's global salvation plans had to be nipped in the bud, lest it spread to infect the rest of the people.

All this helps to introduce us to more keys to spiritual success . . .

1. Give God the firstfruits

God gave his bride her promised home. She lived in it though she did not build it. She harvested what she never planted. She drank of the grapes that she had never nurtured.

'All this is yours,' God said in essence. 'Just give me the firstfruits – Jericho. Make me your first choice when you budget. I don't want your loose change, nor the spare seconds of your day, nor the last ounces of jaded energy.'

This came to mind on disembarking from the El Al plane at Manchester. Small foreign coins can't be changed back into English money, and many of us tossed our left-over shekels into the 'good cause' bin.

'Don't you dare treat me like a charity case,' God seemed to say as the shekels jingled. 'Not after all I've given you.'

In Israel's case, the 'all' was impressive. The Lord got Jericho, and the bride got everything else. Not a bad bargain. Even the wealth of Ai, eventually. Once Achan's sin had been dealt with, the Lord organised a massive victory over Ai and neighbouring Bethel.

After a quarter of the century as a Christian, I'm still amazed by God's generosity. He gives me talents, energy, a body and a mind. Use them, he says. Just give me the firstfruits. In the Old Testament, God's law defined the firstfruits as a tithe – a tenth. Just think! We can keep 90 per cent. Of course, in the New Testament, we're under love. Love always goes more than the mere law. Yet still, we keep the vast majority of the wealth that the Lord gives to us.

2. Give God a clean conscience

I have that magician's trick of making thin silk handkerchiefs disappear into thin air – or rather, into the tip of my false thumb.

But I can also make things vanish in my mind. Sometimes I can be really clever and hide things there without even letting myself know I'm doing it. As you know (here I assume no reader has yet attained sainthood) this is a natural gift with all of us. It comes ready-packed with our original sin.

However, some of us are more 'gifted' than others. Achan was a pastmaster. He had been told not to plunder. His goal should have been to satisfy God's desires rather than his own. But he took and buried the treasure, and then tucked away the criminality of his action in his mental hideaway.

'It'll be okay for me,' he no doubt thought. 'Plenty for God. He'll not miss the odd shekel, and what does he want with a robe? And anyway, it's not really all that wrong. If I don't take it, somebody else will . . . and even if it is sin, there are others doing things a thousand times worse. God'll understand. I've been this way since I was born. It's my weakness, my natural bent.'

Achan's appetites and desires blinded him, seared his conscience, and threatened a whole nation.

A lesbian friend phoned the other night.

'Look at it from my point of view,' she pleaded. 'I was born this way. It's my natural way. It's not really wrong.' God, it seems, didn't really mean to ban homosexuality. The Bible got it wrong. God's prophets got mixed up. The Hebrew nation was mistaken. So too was the apostle Paul, along with every Christian generation in the last two thousand years.

'And just because God made it physically difficult for two women to make love,' my friend added, 'is no reason to assume that he didn't mean it to happen.'

Desires can have such might that only they are right. Everything and everybody else is wrong (Prov 11:6; Mk 4:19; Rom 8:5; 13:4; Gal 5:17).

3. Give God a repentant heart

I often wonder what happened eternally to Achan and his family, not to mention his New Testament counterparts Ananias and Sapphira. Achan did, after all, confess and repent (Josh 7:20). The New Testament couple were described as believers (Acts 5:1–11). I'm even one of those who hope Judas managed to get right with God as he struggled on his tree.

I fear the worst. Then, I thank God that their eternal

destination is not up to me. There, but for the grace of God, go I.

My conversion came through an Ulster vicar who specialised in repentance preaching. It was unfortunate. At least, I thought so at the beginning. I became truly convicted about those longer-than-usual breaks at work. Then, there were the times I had knocked off early when nobody was looking. The day after I resigned to start theological college, my wife and I sent my superannuation cheque back to my old employers. Repentance in my case meant repayment. It was a huge amount, especially with no wage due for the following two years.

'The Lord will provide,' said Linda. And he did.

That lesson is reinforced by the 99.9 per cent of Hebrews who waited for Ai. They got far more than Achan ever did.

Covenant renewed

Just outside Shechem, about thirty miles north of Jericho and Jerusalem, there is a beautiful valley. It is two miles wide, and flanked by Mount Ebal and Mount Gerizim. It's an amazing, natural auditorium. You can stand on one mountain and talk to somebody on the other. The acoustics are crystal clear.

After Ai, Joshua knew that Israel needed to renew their pledges to God, and so he brought them as pilgrims to this lovely vale (Josh 8:30–35).

On Ebal he built an altar by the Book, following God's specifications (in Deuteronomy 27 and 28), and offered burnt sacrifices.

In that incredible amphitheatre, he then read out to all the people – half in front of the green wooded Gerizim and the other half before the barren Ebal – all the words written in the Books of the Law.

These included the blessings of knowing God and the curses of living without him.

Together, they worshipped the God of the second chance, and the third, and fourth, and on and on and on. Nestling in the heart of the Promised Land, the bride made up to the bridegroom.

And together they lived . . . .

16

The Crowning

Our book isn't red. Its size is too small. I'm not Michael Aspel but, 'Joshua, son of Nun and Mum, this is your life!'

Picture the studio. It is beyond heaven's gates. We are coming to the end of the presentation, and already seated are the heroes of heaven. Many of them have paraded their testimony before a heavenly Aspel to celebrate our great warrior leader.

Joshua sits centre-stage, a spectacle before the whole universe. He's here to receive his crowning reward. Around the podium, his peers and God make up the presentation party. They bear the glittering crowns prepared for all victorious warriors. For Joshua. Even for you and me.

Crowns and spectacles

Paul writes about being made a 'spectacle' before the whole universe, angels as well as humanity. In the battle of life, they are like the condemned in the victory parade of a returning hero (1 Cor 4:9).

But eternity will ensure that the soldiers of Christ have their own victory parade to collect their reward. It will not be a perishable red photo album entitled *This Is Your Life*, but an everlasting crown (1 Cor 9:25). It is this parade that we strive to imagine in this chapter.

The people you have helped to save, like Joshua's witnesses, will be your joy and crown (Phil 4:1).

For those who have 'fought the good fight', who have 'finished the race' and 'kept the faith', there is a crown of righteousness (2 Tim 4:7–8).

Elsewhere in Scripture, it is the crown of life, of glory and honour, a crown of lovingkindness, that no man can take away.

It is a crown of gold (Rev 4:4).

The welcome party

Present are some of his old enemies from Canaan and even Jericho; those who at the last moment repented and reached into the wrath of God to touch the giant heart of forgiving love.

For a start, there's faithful Rahab, already wearing her crown. She bears another for her earthly saviour. Her grateful family are there too.

'We can't thank Joshua enough,' her presence says. Her shortened anecdote includes, 'His spies told me to fly a cord, scarlet as blood, from my outer wall window, and the wrath of God would pass over and leave me and my family safe. After the walls fell, he sent in his people to bring us out' (Josh 6:22).

There, too, in the assembled throng is Moses, his own head wreathed in sparkling crowns. There is no trace of his earthly stammer in his imagined testimony: 'Believe me, behind every great man there's a Joshua. Manage without him, I could not. I ask you, my friend, what man is it who buries his own obvious leadership qualities in the prime of life? He put himself last to ensure that I succeeded. Is that a man of God, or what?'

The con artists

To one side, there's a bunch of canny con men, the Gibeonites. They still wait to present Joshua with a crown. It is inscribed, 'For being everything we were not: honest and full of integrity.' Their speech is already prepared: 'A lesser mortal would have run us through with iron javelins after what we did to him. Yet, he was such an honourable man. Even after we tricked him into signing a treaty with us, he marched north and came to our rescue. He even made the sun stand still while he helped beat off our enemies. We were up against 300,000 infantry, 10,000 cavalry and 20,000 war chariots, and he still kept his word, even though we extracted it from him with our false words.'[1]

Was that a sad smile on Joshua's face as he looked at the Gibeonites? Could he be remembering that it was yet another disaster of Ai proportions? Was he kicking himself for yet again failing to listen to God? After Ai, he and Israel had repented and renewed their holy covenant with the Lord at Shechem.

'Of course,' they stressed, 'we'll listen only to you in future, Lord. Honest!'

A short time afterwards they were back on the repentance trail, after listening to the fanciful Gibeonites rather than God.

Con men of Gibeon

The scallywags from Gibeon – a city just up the road from Ai – arrived at Joshua's camp claiming to have travelled 'from a very distant country' to make a treaty.

They put on a convincing show featuring donkeys 'loaded with worn-out sacks and old wineskins, cracked and mended'. The travel-worn image was further enhanced by the men's 'patched sandals', 'old clothes' and bread that was 'dry and mouldy'.

The final touch was clever. They arrived after the victories at Jericho and Ai, yet spoke only of knowing Israel's distant feats in Egypt and the wilderness. This, they claimed, was what made them set off from their 'far country'.

Joshua again forgot to ask his Lord. He listened only to the Gibeonites. He signed a treaty of protection, swearing an oath to the God of Israel.

It is the mark of a great man to keep his word and oath under such circumstances.

Incidentally, the Gibeonites did not wholly escape Joshua's judgement. He made them Israel's servants, and gave their city to the tribe of Benjamin (Josh 18:25).

Old friends . . .

In the heavenly crowd also is Caleb. 'Hi, Hoshea! Fancy a spy like you becoming Ya-hoshea. Remember the day they nearly stoned us to death?'

Alongside Caleb are thousands. Could they possibly be those who survived babyhood simply because Joshua's invasion stifled Molech and child sacrifice? There also are the priests who walked into the raging torrent with the ark of the covenant.

'Do you remember what we thought of Joshua as we dipped our toes in?' one might have said to another. 'But he was right!'

. . . and family

Among the heavenly host are also tribal leaders from the east bank of the Jordan extolling their kinsman's wise, flexible leadership in letting them settle there. Alongside, there are those from the west bank who followed him all the days of their lives and for a generation beyond.

'And not only this,' any of the assembled might have said, 'but he presided superbly over the division of the Promised Land. Having done this, he gave us our title deeds [Josh 13–21] so that we could all know for certain which lands the Lord had given to us.'

The tribal leaders on the east – the Reubenites, Gadites and half the tribe of Manasseh – could express especial gratitude for Joshua's inspiration, even though it nearly brought civil war. As Promised Land peace took the place of strife, Joshua had summoned the two and a half tribes who had led the way:

> You have not deserted your brothers but have carried out the mission the Lord your God gave you . . . . Return to your homes . . . on the other side of the Jordan. But be very careful to keep the commandment and the law that Moses the servant of the Lord gave you: to love the Lord your God, to walk in all his ways, to obey his commands, to hold fast to him and to serve him with all your heart and all your soul (Josh 22:3–5).

The leaders of the tribes were eager to fulfil this command. More so, because the Jordan seemed to cut them off from their brothers. That's why they decided to build an altar on their side of the Jordan. It was to stand as a witness to the fact that they too served the same God.

The west bank tribes mistook this as a declaration of spiritual independence. They feared the wrath of God on all Israel, and were prepared to fight the east bank tribes. At the last moment they held peace talks, and came to understand that the altar was merely a replica of the main one in Israel.

Joshua had taught them well. They had communicated. They had listened to each other. They had shared. They had recognised that each side of the Jordan was doing its utmost for the same highest God. They had ended up thoroughly appreciating each other.

Guest of honour

In our heavenly *This Is Your Life* studio, there's a special place of honour. There stands the Commander of the Lord's Army welcoming home his earthly general. With him are the heavenly strategists.

The man who was 'Q'

I enjoy imagining a more modern saint joining the heavenly strategists, and no doubt bending Joshua's ear. He is my old and late friend Charles Fraser-Smith.

The tactics of Joshua and other Old Testament heroes helped Charles in his role as the real secret service 'Q' during World War II. The 'Q', incidentally, comes from the James Bond books, written by Ian Fleming, whose Naval Intelligence office was in the next building to that of Fraser-Smith.

Charles was forever talking and writing about how the Joshuas of Scripture helped us beat the enemy.[2] The reason was quite simple: the men who made modern allied strategy were themselves influenced by such biblical heroes.

Field Marshal Montgomery came from a missionary family and read the Bible daily. Lieutenant-General Sir William Dobbie, defender of Malta, carried round a pocket Bible. So too did Chief of Staff General Sir Arthur Smith. Major-General Orde Wingate drove vastly superior forces out of Ethiopia and later led the Chindits in Burma 'pistol in one hand and Bible in the other'. Other God-fearing Biblemen were General Eisenhower, Field Marshal Viscount Alanbrooke, Air Chief Marshal Sir Wilfrid Freeman. Winston Churchill certainly had an excellent working knowledge of Scripture.[3]

The man who was 'Q' thoroughly approved of Joshua's conquest of Canaan, and he himself used many biblical ideas in equipping our secret agents during the war.

□□□

'Well done, Joshua,' the strategists might have chorused. 'We couldn't have done it better ourselves.'

The victories of Jericho, Ai and against the foes of the Gibeonites effectively drove a wedge into the heart of Canaan. The tribe of Judah then drove south while Joshua and his forces moved north and on to the coastal plains. Effectively, it caught the remainder of Canaan in a nut-cracker-like pincer movement.

The refugees

Certainly present in heaven are some of the many who owed their lives to the justice of Joshua and his refuge plan (Josh 20:1–9).

Israel had no Scotland Yard. Detection and punishment were in the hands of a victim's nearest male relative, which obviously had its problems.

In the case of killings – quite numerous in primitive societies – high emotions did not always make a distinction between deliberate murder and unintentional manslaughter. Joshua had therefore set aside certain cities where asylum for accidental killers could be found.

Refuge or prison?

Even innocent manslaughter was regarded as a major fault by Israel, points out H. L. Ellison in his Scripture Union book on Joshua. The law protected the innocent man but nevertheless heavily penalised him.

He had to leave home and stay within about half a mile

of his refuge city (Num 35:26–27). It was more like a prison than anything else, especially if the manslaughterer knew only farming. Many might even have been reduced to begging, but at least they kept their lives.

Release came when the high priest of the day died. That signalled a general amnesty. Refuges were probably stop-gap justice centres in early Israel. They fell into disuse once society became more central and civilised.

And now Joshua's crowning ceremony reaches its climax . . . .

Notes

[1] Joshua 10. The statistics come from the historian Josephus, as quoted by Paul Enns, *Joshua*, p 96.

[2] Charles Fraser-Smith with Kevin Logan, *Secret Warriors, Hidden Heroes of MI6, OSS, SOE & SAS* (Paternoster Press).

[3] Charles Fraser-Smith, *Men of Faith* (Paternoster Press).

17
For Divine Service

And so, with the witnesses assembled, we come to the crowning of Joshua – God's Old Testament saviour.

'For services rendered . . . ' is often the phrase that precedes an investiture. But this is a heavenly presentation. We need divine words. Those God gave to Joshua just before leaving Israel at the grand old age of 110 will do just fine.

The citation, taken from the essence of Joshua chapter 23, might go something like this:

> For being strong, and very courageous; for obeying God's word and urging others to do so . . . (v 6).

Joshua always concentrated on the positive. The godly life was never just a question of avoiding evil but of doing good. The citation goes on:

> For turning neither left nor right from God's way, and urging others to follow in his footsteps, especially avoiding diversions offered by others . . . (v 7).

Israel had similar multicultural diversions to ourselves today. To be politically correct, we are required to accept other religions, and try to find where God is in them. To be theologically correct, Joshua simply said, 'Do not associate with these nations that remain among you; do not invoke the names of their gods or swear by them. You must not serve them or bow down to them' (Josh 23:7).

Compromise is the ever-present peril whatever the age, but especially for God's bride.

Almost as soon as he carried her over the threshold of the Jordan she had begun to flirt with the local playboy god called Baal. She saw him as the big-spender type. He seemed to provide all his worshippers' needs.

Baal was always there in her most vulnerable times, especially when life was hard and she was having second thoughts. Sure, her husband might have worked wonders during the desert honeymoon. He was certainly a good breadwinner. The daily delivery of manna bread had proved that. But how would he measure up in the new situation in Canaan? It was a whole new lifestyle. Previously, wandering Israel had thought the ground was made for walking on. Now she had to dig it – or die! She sometimes felt as much at home down on the farm as a burly Liverpool docker picking daisies.

Israel's husband might conjure up bread, but could he be trusted to produce a thousand fields of corn? And what of the hundreds of vegetable patches, not to mention vineyards? All that and more would be needed to keep hunger and thirst at bay. Her life was at stake. The bright boy Baal, on the other hand, had already proved himself, she reckoned. The land overflowed with good food. No kitchen pantry was empty. Plenty for everyone.

Israel was tempted to walk out on her husband there and then and throw in her lot with Baal. However, she played it smart. She kept God as her husband and made Baal her lover.

We play the same religious insurance game. You put your money on God for hatches, matches, dispatches,

Easter, Christmas and Sundays. After all, they're his speciality. But when it comes to a new model Ford Fiesta for the wife, or even a new model to replace the wife, you bank on the god of materialism.

Israel's version, of course, concerned more basic things. She kept her hubby safe and happy in the background with a few prayers and sacrifices. But when it came to the bread-and-butter issues of daily living, she ran to her lover, Baal.

Rain, as we noted earlier, was Israel's most vital need. A long hot summer could last for years, and if anyone could promise a downpour, he was an immediate favourite. Baal did. To Israel, it was as tempting as a crate of Pepsi in the middle of the Negev desert.

Joshua's crowning citation continues:

> For showing us God as someone who loves us, and someone whom we can love in return (v 11).

Pre-Moses, it was a little difficult to see how anyone could have a loving relationship with this God of Abraham, Isaac and Jacob. He didn't seem to do much, and a life of slavery in Egypt was no great testament to his care.

Post-Joshua, Israel was in no doubt about the God who cared. He could part seas and rivers for his beloved people, feed them in a wilderness for a generation, and bring robust walls and mighty enemies crashing before him.

This was no distant deity. This was a loving God who rolled up his sleeves and got stuck in to the daily difficulties of coping with one of the most inhospitable wildernesses in the world. Then, when he settled his people in a new land, he stayed around to deal with the world's greatest political hot-spot.[1]

Finally, Joshua would receive his crown:

> For making crystal clear the only successful option open to humanity (Josh 24).

This option came in three parts.

First, '*Choose for yourselves this day whom you will serve, whether the gods your forefathers served . . .*' (Josh 24:15 my italics).

This is the choice British society is making today. Paganism and the occult have massively increased throughout society in the past decade.[2] At the time of going to press the BBC's *Everyman* programme labels Paganism as 'the fastest growing religion in Britain.' Paganism and the occult feature in practically every outlet of the High Street – book and video shops, newsagents, cinemas, children's toy stores, libraries, criminal courts, computer centres, New Age alternatives, music departments, and so on.

Amazing, isn't it, that educated, sophisticated, intelligent post-modern man is reaching for his stars or keying into the Internet to tell his fortune?

Just before writing this book, I was researching sects and cults for *Twisted Truth*, published by the Evangelical Alliance. We estimated upwards of a thousand new religious movements in Britain at present. Other experts in the field suggested there were as many as 3,000 new groups.

There's a second option facing humanity in search of something to worship.

'*Choose for yourselves this day whom you will serve . . .*' *challenged Joshua,* '*whether the gods . . . of the Amorites, in whose land you are living*' (Josh 24:15 my italics).

The Israelites had the choice of following the gods of the people whom they had conquered.

The god of our culture is still very much materialism and scientism. The intellectuals of Canaan offered a similar god.

'Do this sex ritual with a prostitute and make certain child sacrifices and you will get rain and good crops and prosperity,' preached the high priests of Baal and Molech. 'If you do nothing, then nothing happens on the farm.'

It was a mechanical religion run on laboratory cause-and-effect lines.

Modern materialism and scientism are similar. The world is reduced to a mechanism. A human being is part of it, merely a chemical-electric ape. Gods in white coats tell us that one day we will know enough to control our climate once and for all. One day we really will know which are the right laboratory rituals. One day, we'll even perfect birth control so that we don't have to sacrifice any more babies to maintain our comfortable lifestyles.

Third, says Joshua, '*Choose for yourselves . . . . But as for me and my household, we will serve the Lord*' (Josh 24:15 my italics).

As I have studied the rise in new and alternative spiritualities over the last decade, there has been an interesting development. The yearly increase in new groups shows that men and women, especially those young and idealistic, are fleeing the modern age of materialism and technology.

They have experienced the death of their souls in an arid mechanistic era. Within, they know that the gods of yesterday are useless. Now, there is a revolution under way in our society. We are leaving behind the modern days – the Age of Reason and Enlightenment. We are in search of something new.

'As for me and my children,' the young are saying, 'we will serve . . . .'

And then they come to a hesitant halt. They are left to flit from option to option, seeking, though rarely finding. They are butterflies fluttering by in a desert trying to find the real blooms that give life.

Not for years has there been such a spiritually hungry mood in the nation. They want to serve something . . . somebody . . . worth serving.

The Lord waits for more Joshuas to cry out, 'As for me and my household/church/family/fellowship/denomination, we will serve the Lord.'

And a crown awaits every one who does so.

God needs more Joshuas. He needs people who will be his saviours in a lost world.

As for me and my family . . . .

Notes

[1] Joshua 24 gives a beautiful summary of the Lord's deeds for Israel.

[2] I have set out my research in three books – *Paganism and the Occult*, *Close Encounters with the New Age* and *Satanism and the Occult* – all published by Kingsway and Reachout Trust.

Study Guide

by Hilary Price

1: Saviour?

1. What did the spies report they had seen in Israel (Num 13:26–29)?
2. What conclusions did they draw from what they saw?
   – Joshua and Caleb (Num 13:30)?
   – The other ten spies (Num 13:31, 33)?
3. Why did they see the same things and react differently?
4. What effect does the report of the ten spies have on the rest of the camp?
5. What is God's view of grumbling (Num 14:26–30, 36–38)?
6. Caleb is described as 'a man with a different spirit' (Num 14:24). What is different about the way he and Joshua see God and therefore the situation around them?

2: Saviour in the Making

1. Joshua grew up knowing certain truths (p27). What were they? What truths did you grow up knowing and how have they influenced your outlook on life?
2. What had Joshua as Moses' assistant seen of the character of God?

3. What had God taught Joshua through the battle with the Amalekites (Ex 17:8–16)?
4. Who have you looked up to as a mentor or leader in your life?
5. Can you recall a time when you had to lead alone – just you and God? Were you prepared or just flung in at the deep end? In what way had Joshua been prepared for the responsibility that lay ahead?
6. How does God reassure Joshua (Josh 1:5)?

3: Parable from Hell

1. What gods do societies create for themselves? Why do we do this?
2. Why would a family be willing to sacrifice one of its children?
3. Do you think drought is a form of punishment?
4. If ' . . . what may be known about God is plain' (Rom 1:19), why is there such diversity and confusion in understanding who God is and what he does?
5. 'They exchanged the truth of God for a lie . . .' (Rom 1:25). What was the truth and what was the lie?
6. Do you think abortion is the modern equivalent of the child sacrifice made to the god Molech in the days of Joshua (Jer 32:35)?

4: God's No Devil

1. Is war ever right?
2. Why do we not like to associate God with war?
3. How is the wrath of God being revealed on the world (Rom 2:5–11)?
4. Who provokes God's wrath (Rom 2:5–11)?
5. Is God's wrath ever directed towards Christians (Jn 3:36; Rom 5:8–11)?
6. 'For God does not show favouritism' (Rom 2:11). How

does this statement tie in with the divine ethnic cleansing of the Promised Land to make room for the Israelites (Deut 20:16–18)?

5: Secrets of Success

1. Why did God command Joshua three times to be strong and very courageous in Joshua 1?
2. God gave Joshua instructions about what to 'be' and also about what to 'do'. What were these instructions (Josh 1:7b–8)?
3. What kind of prosperity and success results from meditating on the Bible day and night (Josh 1:8)?
4. Can you recall a time when you have really known God with you 'as he was with Moses'?
5. Who else springs to mind in Scripture as someone who very obviously knew and relied upon God as the present I AM?
6. How would you describe your prayer life? Why do you think it is like it is?
7. What do you learn about leadership from observing Joshua's behaviour before he led the people across the River Jordan?

6: Myth or Miracle?

1. Why do people prefer to interpret Bible events as myths rather than miracles; fables rather than facts?
2. 'God has to be bigger than our heads' (p70). What do you think this means?
3. List Joshua's six secrets.
4. What makes him so sure of these secrets? Look at each one and work out when he learned that particular secret and how God embedded it in his heart.
5. Look again at the list of secrets. Which could you claim to share? Why?

6. Knowing is one thing and doing is another. When we know amazing truths about God, why do we so often find it difficult to live in the good of these truths and step out in the power of them? How might we help ourselves to do that?

7: Moving God's People

1. 'God gives a little. We use well. God gives more' (p75). Can you think of other characters in Scripture whose lives illustrate this principal? Would you conclude that God gives 'a little' to a certain type of person?
2. Are you encouraged or discouraged by Joshua? Can you explain your response?
3. What part do 'good works' play in the Christian life (Lk 18:19; Jas 2:14–26; Rom 2:6–7; Eph 2:10; Mt 5:16)?
4. 'One of our greatest motivations is the realisation of what God has freed us from' (p79). What are you thankful God has freed you from? What do you find it hard to let go of?
5. What does it mean, in practical terms, to 'submit yourself to God'?
6. Can you identify failures in your life which still influence you and prevent you from moving on?

8: The Calling

1. Have you ever stood on God's launch pad? How did you get there and what happened?
2. Who in Scripture stepped out of ' . . . his will and into his own' (p87)? Unfortunately there are plenty to choose from (e.g. Adam and Eve, Abraham, David etc.)! What were the results?
3. 'You want a life! Get a calling' (p89). Do you know God's calling on your life? Did it come gradually or in

an instant? If you do not have a specific calling do you think you should have? How would you go about discovering what it is?

4. Is guidance your responsibility or God's (Prov 3:5–6)?
5. Look up 1 Corinthians 1:27. Why does God use weak people?
6. From Chapter 8, what are the most important principles you have learned about how and why God calls a person for his purposes? Has his strategy changed? How do you know?

9: Take It or Leave It

1. When there is such interest in the supernatural, why is it hard to explain miracles to people of this day and age?
2. Why did Joshua spell out that crossing the Jordan involved a miracle?
3. What other key events in the Bible can only be explained by 'God did it'?
4. What was the purpose of erecting a wayside memorial once the Israelites had crossed the Jordan?
5. Compare the crossing of the Jordan (Josh 3:7–17; 4:15–18) with the crossing of the Exodus sea (Ex 14:13–31). Are there any similarities which teach principles about the way God works?
6. Why did God use Moses and Joshua in these particular events? Does he need a person when performing miracles? Refer to Old and New Testament miracles to come up with an answer.

10: How to Manage – Part 1

1. 'The first rule of life management . . . Get the vision of where you are going. Rule number two: share the vision with others' (p106). Do you agree that this approach is crucial in the church and in the home? Think of some

practical ways in which these rules are worked out in your church and your home.
2. Why do many leaders find it hard to delegate?
3. What are the difficulties of teamwork?
4. What are the values of teamwork?
5. What qualities of good leadership are shown in the way Joshua deals with the three million Israelites?
6. 'Leaders are born, not made.' Do you agree with this statement? Do you think leadership can be taught to or drawn out of individuals? What warnings does God give leaders? How can you train a leader? Look at 1 Samuel 7:5–6; 1 Samuel 12:1–2; 2 Samuel 23:3; Isaiah 3:14; 10:1; Romans 12:4–8.

11: How to Manage – Part 2

1. Why do you think the people were willing to do what Joshua commanded even though the instructions seemed so bizarre (Josh 6:6–11)?
2. 'Worry your problems into solutions and you will have success' (p120). Do you agree? Can you give an everyday illustration of this idea?
3. How does giving my utmost for his highest and working at peak efficiency tie in with 1 Corinthians 1:27, 'God chose the foolish things of the world . . . God chose the weak things of this world to shame the strong'?
4. Is encouragement a gift for a few or the responsibility of everyone (Rom 12:3–8)?
5. Why is encouragement so important for individuals and for teams? What effect does it have (Acts 20:1–3; 2 Sam 19:1–8)?
6. Who has been a Barnabas (son of encouragement) in your life?
7. How could you be more of an encourager
   – in your church?
   – at work?

- in your family?
- in your marriage?
- among your friends?

12: A Few Home Truths

1. Have you ever had to submit to a leader who 'knows what he is doing', even when you didn't agree? What happened?
2. Why was it necessary for Joshua and the Israelites to wait at Gilgal for three days before 'taking' Jericho?
3. 'Woe to those who say, "Let God hurry"' (Is 5:19). Can you think of instances and reasons elsewhere in Scripture when God made people wait?
4. It is unlikely that our whole nation will repent. But what of your family? Our confession might go something like this . . .

   We repent of (a)
   (b)
   (c)

   Fill in the gaps.
5. In what ways does God want us to 'become like little children' (Lk 18:15–17)?
6. Which 'grown-ups' in the Bible showed childlike faith?
7. Is it hard to go through the 'trust barrier' (p133)? Why?

13: God Loves Prostitutes

1. What is God's attitude to sin (Rom 6:23; 14:23; 1 Tim 1:15; 1 Jn 1:9; Heb 8:12; Lk 5:24; 2 Cor 5:21)?
2. What is God's attitude to sinners (Lk 15:7; 1 Pet 3:18; 4:8; Mt 1:21)?
3. What should be our attitude to sin (Mk 9:43; Heb

12:1; 1 Jn 1:8; Rom 6:14; Prov 23:17; Jas 5:16; Gal 5:16–17)?
4. What should be our attitude to sinners (Jn 8:7; Mt 6:15; Jn 20:23; Gal 6:1–2)?
5. God hates sin but not the sinner. Why do we so often hate the sinner?
6. Why had a 'great fear fallen on the land' according to Rahab (Josh 2:9–13)?

14: Beware Success!

1. 'Apparent success or the fear of failure are the chief causes of Christian disobedience. The first makes us run faster than we should. The last makes us run away' (p146). How is this illustrated in the lives of some of the other 'greats' (e.g. Moses, David, Saul, Elijah etc.)?
2. Achan was only one among thousands. Why did his sin matter so much to God?
3. Why had Joshua stopped listening to God?
4. What is the danger of success?
5. What is 'success' from God's point of view?
6. Can you think of a time when you have gone it alone, not listened to God and then had to live with the consequences in your life and in the lives of others?

15: The Stoning

1. 'A society that is easy on sin will sin with ease' (p153). In what way does that describe your country today? Can you be specific?
2. Why was Achan's sin dealt with so severely?
3. Do you 'struggle with Achan's stoning' (p154)?
4. Does God punish sin today?
5. What offerings are unacceptable to God and what offerings are acceptable to God (Hos 8:11–14; 1 Chron 21:24; Amos 5:21–27; Mal 1:6–11)?

6. Does God still want a tenth as he did in the Old Testament (Mal 3:10; Rom 12:1; Heb 13:15–16)?
7. What are you tempted to withhold from God?

16: The Crowning

1. What types of crown are 'available' (1 Cor 9:24–27)?
2. What crowns did Jesus wear (Jn 19:1–5; Heb 2:6–9b; Rev 14:14; 19:11–12)?
3. Who will receive a crown (2 Tim 4:8; Jas 1:12; Rev 2:10)?
4. What will the elders do with their crowns (Rev 4: 10–11)?
5. Apparently modern-day leaders have been inspired by Bible commanders. You may not head up an army, but which Bible character has inspired you in what you do?
6. What do you think about Joshua's treatment of those guilty of manslaughter?

17: For Divine Service

1. 'Compromise is the ever-present peril whatever the age . . . ' (p170). How is it possible to accept people of other religions without accepting their religion?
2. What tempts people to forsake the one true God and worship other gods?
3. What would you see as an expression of God's love for you in your life?
4. 'You know with all your heart and soul that not one of all the good promises the Lord your God gave you has failed. Every promise has been fulfilled' (Josh 23:14). What promises of God
   – do you know?
   – have you seen fulfilled?
   – are you banking on?
5. 'But as for me and my household, we will serve the

Lord' (Josh 24:15b). Is this true of you? Who or what are you tempted to serve other than God?

6. How do you express your service to God in daily life
   – as an individual?
   – as a family?
7. From all you have read in the story of Joshua and thought about through this book, what has
   – challenged you most?
   – rebuked you most?
   – encouraged you most?
   – inspired you most?
8. Finish this sentence: 'I would consider my life had been a success if . . . .'

Index of Panels

Index of Life Issues

Elijah: Anointed and Stressed

by Jeff Lucas

ELIJAH – a leader called by God, a hero of the faith, champion of God's cause, fearless opponent of the forces of evil. A man racked by self-doubt, stressed out and ready to give up.

YOU know that you have been called by God to stand for him in a slick and cynical age, to be unpopular when necessary, yet to attract people to the Christian faith. If you're honest, you're not sure how much longer you can hold it together. Let Elijah's story encourage you. Welcome to reality, where victory stems from honest appraisal, not denial.

'There is always trouble when truth is allowed to creep into Christianity. Jeff Lucas is a troublemaker and this book is excellent. Anyone involved in Christian work would do well to read it.'

– ADRIAN PLASS

'Elijah's passion and remarkable obedience to God have been captured by Jeff Lucas in this imaginative book. The combination of narrative and teaching make it hard to put down.'

– GERALD COATES

JEFF LUCAS is a speaker and Bible teacher with an international ministry. He works alongside the Pioneer Team and the Evangelical Alliance. He and his wife Kay live with their family in Chichester.

Elisha: A Sign and a Wonder

by Greg Haslam

ELISHA didn't just make pronouncements on the spiritual climate of his age – he brought about a change. He was a thermostat, not a thermometer. A man with a prophetic edge that translated into a miracle ministry.

YOU are in a society with declining values. Relationships are as polluted as the environment; commitment is seen as fanaticism. Let Elisha's story inspire you to reform society, not reflect it; to 'dig ditches' to water the land and bring revival to a thirsty nation.

'Do you need to recover your cutting edge; see that there are more with you than against you; discover that there is always enough fresh oil for you? Then bring your empty vessel to Greg's faithful and excellent exposition of these matchless stories of Elisha and you will not be disappointed.'

– TERRY VIRGO

GREG HASLAM is Pastor of the Winchester Family Church in Hampshire, where his powerful Bible exposition has helped to revolutionise the lives of many in his local community.

Moses: The Making of a Leader

by Cleland Thom

MOSES began life in deep water – and there he might have stayed. But God had a unique role for him to play, and the leadership training course he devised made sure Moses was fit for that role.

YOU know that you are not yet the leader God wants you to be, but you are prepared to be trained. Let the story of Moses inspire you to a new level of dedication and service.

'Cleland Thom is a good storyteller. The early life of Moses is the story of a man taken out of useful mediocrity and shaped into a leader. If ever we needed leaders in all sections of society it is now. That is why this book is so important.'

– GERALD COATES

CLELAND THOM is a journalist and lecturer in journalism. He is also the author of *The Power to Persuade* and (with Jeff Lucas) *Friends of God*.